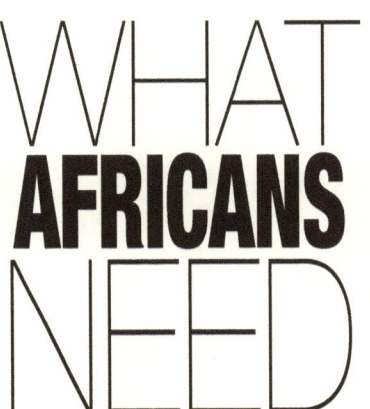

WHAT
AFRICANS
NEED

WHAT AFRICANS NEED

CHUKWUEMEKA E. ONYEJINDUAKA

authorHOUSE®

AuthorHouse™
1663 Liberty Drive
Bloomington, IN 47403
www.authorhouse.com
Phone: 1-800-839-8640

Published by AuthorHouse   02/11/2013

ISBN: 978-1-4817-8149-7 (sc)
ISBN: 978-1-4817-8148-0 (hc)
ISBN: 978-1-4817-8150-3 (e)

Any people depicted in stock imagery provided by Thinkstock are models, and such images are being used for illustrative purposes only.
Certain stock imagery © Thinkstock.

This book is printed on acid-free paper.

Because of the dynamic nature of the Internet, any web addresses or links contained in this book may have changed since publication and may no longer be valid. The views expressed in this work are solely those of the author and do not necessarily reflect the views of the publisher, and the publisher hereby disclaims any responsibility for them.

CONTENTS

CHAPTER ONE

COMMITMENT

Commitment is the power behind every victory, it provokes victory and puts it ahead of defeat. Nobody wins a battle without commitment and nobody realizes a vision without commitment. Commitment is a key that unlocks all the doors of victory and progressive living. Life without commitment is worthless, absolute death, and spiritual deformity.

Commitment can be seen as anger in the mind of a provoked person who is ready to fight and win. In another perspective commitment is a visionalized victory in a winning man who has refused to fail. One can also see commitment as the eyes that see victory in the future.

If the definitions of commitment can be seen as aforementioned, it therefore means that commitment should be considered as an ingrate part of life as it is. No commitment, no life; no life, no commitment. Whatsoever one is not committed to, such,

1

he will never have. When a person is totally committed to his vision, such vision will not die. When a person is committed to his vision such individual will not rest until the vision is realized. commitment is of different hierarchies and views, hence, people see it differently. While a lot of people are committed to air vision and their visions die before they are born, some others are committed to what is called water vision, hence, they initiate unstable projects.

WHAT IS AIR/WATER VISION

These are the visions considered as dreaming great dreams inside a dream. The question you ask a person who is sleeping and having a dream, and right inside the same dream he begins to have another dream, which of these dreams will be realized first? When a person is hoping to get the impossible done in a few seconds, such individual is having an air vision. Any vision conceived while flying in the air cannot be realized. How can one conceive a vision while flying in the air?

In Africa, most of the leaders do have a lot of visions for the people during their political rallies without knowing how to realize them. Any vision conceived, but the visioner did not know how to realize it, is considered as air vision. Water vision can be likened to a vision that is beyond the control of the visioner, which automatically gives access to people, for a person to say he/she has a vision it means that the visioner must have found solution to such vision. If otherwise, people will then come in to decide the fate of such vision, therefore, whichever way it goes, the visioner conceived water vision.

Considering air and water vision you will discover that it takes a committed heart to conceive a reasonable vision for the people. It takes a man/woman of spiritual and physical commitment to conceive a vision and realize such vision for the people. African democracy is not succeeding because it lacks what is called inward commitment. Inward commitment is a situation where one is committed to self development by properly using things that are within in order to get things that are outside, putting all together to enhance the quality of life. You can also see inward commitment as one having good mind that conceived good vision for the people using the same people to realize their vision without struggles and harassment. In Africa, the leaders lack managerial character that can pave way for primary human development and empowerment. African leaders have initiated a lot of good visions, yet, Africans are suffering. From OAU to AU a lot of good programmes have been initiated, still Africans are not satisfied. This is because inward commitment is missing. The leaders are depending on oversea aids and grants to develop Africa, because they believe that without foreign connections Africans cannot succeed. This is lack of self trust.

If African leaders can understand clearly that nobody can help Africa better than Africans they will stop looking for help overseas. Rather they will return home to seek what I call home solution. It is only then that things will begin to work out well. If African leaders can understand that the people of Africa need their fellow Africans to be better, I think Africans will start presenting themselves as good people from a better prospective to the world. Around August 2009, there was news that in a certain African country, Libya to be precise, thousands of Nigerians were facing death sentences and in other African countries a lot of Nigerians have been killed, mostly in South Africa. If Africans can be against their fellow Africans to such extreme, then what does the future hold for Africa. From the lifetime of OAU to AU African leaders have not been able to put in place what I call 'Africa for African protection laws'. This means the following:

- It is a law that tells who an African person is.
- It is a law that tells the level of punishment an African person will not receive outside his/her country as long as Africa is concerned.
- It is a law that determines deportation of Africans who have committed a capital offence in another country.
- It is a law that makes an African feel at home in any part of Africa without harassment.
- It is a law that holds a country responsible for murder of an individual in such country.
- It is a law that is empowered to put it to African leaders that once a person is deported for committing a crime, the country of immigrant should be held responsible if

such individual is thereafter found in the country where he had been deported.

- It is a law that can compel African leaders to stand the risk of paying compensations to a country that deported a person and later such person is found in the country again.

Though a lot of laws have been made to protect the African child the question is are these laws indeed protecting Africans? In the days of OAU, a lot of laws were put in place to protect Africans and to ensure better life for every African, but those laws did not make impact in the lives of ordinary Africans. The reason is that the leaders who put up these laws did not make the laws in the interest of the generality of Africans, rather, the laws were made to ensure their steady stay in office as leaders in their different countries. Though people may have different views over this matter, my position remains that African leaders are not committed to Africans and African projects. It is very easy to convene meetings in Addis Ababa to make laws, but it is not easy to implement these laws, because there are many ways people make laws and there are many ways people can be deceived by such laws. One can make laws to deceive people, and people make laws to control and deceive people as well. One who is in authority can make laws to ensure his stay in office, people can as well make laws to ensure that their positions are well secured. One cannot see any successful programmes put in place by the OAU or AU, except peace keeping forces. Apart from peace keeping which also has international backing like all other programmes, I have not seen any other programme in Africa put in place by African leaders that has stood the test of time and is successful without foreign support.

I was born and brought up in Africa and in my own capacity have been observing certain happenings and have come to realize that the most successful programmes in my country and most African countries were initiated by the UN, my question are:

- What is wrong with Africans?
- What is happening in Africa?
- Don't we have people that can think in Africa?
- Why are we having selfish leaders?
- Why is Africa so dependent?
- Why is Africa so poor?
- Why doesn't Africa have a system of democracy?

After pondering on all these questions one would realize that the answer to these questions is, Africans are not committed to Africans and African projects.

- Without commitment Africans will continue to tread the wrong path, because they are not committed to truth and sincerity.
- Without commitment there will be no good leadership, such are the past happenings that put Africans where they are today and if caution is not taken it will continue.

6

- Without commitment towards ensuring security of lives, good people that can think well will continue to hide or run away from Africa to save their heads. For instance, Africans are happy that Mr. Barrack Obama is elected the first black president of the United states of America, permit me to say that if Barrack Obama was born in Africa he might not become president, perhaps he might have been killed just as they have killed many Obamas in Nigeria or he probably would have ran away from Africa to save his head. This is not to say that there are no vices elsewhere. In a situation where the system is so bad it paves way for bad people to always find their way to the seat of power, thereby making the situation to be worrisome.

- Without commitment Africans will continue to experience bad leadership, the electoral process is too bad making their voting system to be worse than that of the rest of the world. Hence those who have enough money to buy the seat of power will continue to be in power. In Africa, it does not matter whether one has good vision for the people or not, all that matters is that the person who has a lot of money to buy people's conscience has been selected to lead the people, that is why Africans do have election by selection not by voting.

- Africans will continue to depend on Europe and America to succeed, because they are not committed to development. African leaders are not committed to African and her projects, that is why the few in government will always gather themselves to loot the treasury leaving Africans in poverty, making development in Africa impossible.

- Without commitment on issues that matter Africa will remain poor, hence, the poor get poorer and the rich get richer and politics becomes a 'do or die' affair.

- Without commitment there will be no system of democracy. For Africans to have a true system of democracy, deceit will have to stop, this will ensure a better way for true federalism. What Africa therefore needs to develop in every area of life is commitment without which the situation will continue to get worse.

CHAPTER TWO

COMPROMISING LEADERSHIP

Compromising leadership in Africa has become a worrisome issue over the years, it has become an inexplicable situation, it has become a cankerworm experience in African politics. Millions of people have said a lot of things concerning Africa and their system of governance. The only few countries in Africa that are operating or trying to operate true democracy are not encouraging others to be like them, rather they are supporting some of these compromising leaders just to protect their political interest. Anywhere political interest is discussed, know that someone or a group of people who claim to be powerful have selected an individual to suit their desire. Compromising leadership is very deadly, wherever it is found, people suffer a lot without a hope for tomorrow. This is why it is purely based on protecting someone or some people's interest politically to the detriment of the populace.

In Africa, it is only few countries that are practicing pure democracy, while others are practicing what I consider compromising democracy. Nonetheless, those few countries that have decided to do things in a proper way are looking at the so called giant of Africa to act in the right direction, but the so called giant of Africa is doing nothing to correct herself let alone correcting faulty countries. South African democratic structure is of reputable standard, that is why an elected president can afford to resign from office, because he wants the wishes of the people to prevail. In most part of Africa it is not possible for an elected president to willingly resign from office without completing his tenure, rather, he will find a way to change the existing constitution to elongate his tenure, probably unto eternity, because after him his son or daughter will have to continue from where he stopped. In Africa, once a party wins an election such party as a matter of fact becomes an everlasting ruling party, no other party can win election. It is only in Ghana that such a thing is not happening, the wishes of the people prevail. This was a great foundation laid by their former military head of state; Jerry Rawlings who handed over power to an opposition party candidate John Kufur. And after his tenure he handed over to John Atta Mills, another opposition. Ghana's system of politics is similar to that of the US.

Nigeria that claims to be the giant of Africa is operating a one party system, that is, all other people who are holding governorship seats or other posts have to decamp to the everlasting ruling party so as to be 'reselected' in the next 'selection' period, because election in Nigeria ended in 1993. If one is not in the ruling party one can hardly be selected to assume any political seat in Nigeria, for it is not the wishes of the people that prevail, rather, the wishes of some powerful civilians do. It is a case where 3% population of the country who have dubiously enriched themselves come together to enslave the other 97%. Those who are ready to work to ensure that Nigeria have a place in destiny have been killed and those who are alive are afraid. In Nigeria what we are seeing is what I call 'deathocracy', not democracy. What is deathocracy? It is a word given to African system of democracy which is anchored on compromise. South Africa and Ghana are exempted, because the two countries have worked hard to keep their countries' hope of having purely elected leaders in power. Countries like Liberia, Sierra-Leone and Ivory Coast are exempted for now, because their democracy have suffered setbacks due to civil wars and political crisis.

Looking at the countries of Africa you will see that they lack political techniques and sense of political management, meaning that they have totally lost democratic sense thereby subjecting the entire Africans to become pitiful babes. Any part of the world the voice of an African is heard, it is a long plaintive cry for help. The reason for this is that the system of African democracy is focusless, baseless and confused, hence, it is difficult to have credible elections in Africa.

In Nigeria, what we have is selected people inpower, you cannot see anybody in any position that will come out to tell the world that he/she is clearly elected by the people. From the ward counselors to local government chairmen to the state and federal level, virtually nobody was duly elected by the people. Those who were not selected by their political parties may have enough money to buy thugs and steal ballot boxes so as to help them cast the vote of all Nigerians in their houses and eventually declare themselves winners. No matter how you view this issue, the fact is that certain people have helped Nigerians to perform their civil rights in the secret without their consent. At the end of the whole saga whoever that is in charge will go ahead and announce that an individual who did not know what it takes to be a leader has won the election with overwhelming number of votes cast perhaps by all the ghosts in the country. Despite all the political killings taking place in Nigeria, and worthless moves to combat it, the government has not been able to nab and charge any of the killers to court, all we see or hear about are paraded suspects while the real killers always go about their daily activities with impunity, wonders shall never end! If this kind of situation is taking place in the giant of Africa nation, then, what is the reason why Togo Republic and Gabon will not call the first sons of their 'God-sent' presidents that have died to come and continue from where their fathers stopped? The reason is that those countries do not have any other person good enough to be elected as president. Moreso, these countries cannot tell us that they have the type of democracy that is applicable in the civilized world, I tag such system monarchtocracy, which is a system where people operate on a monarchical system of governance in pretence, it is also a system where people are made to believe that a particular group of people are the only people good enough to be selected as president.

In Togo, the people are made to believe that it is only the son of their late president that is good to replace his father. In Gabon, the same took place, therefore, these countries are operating monarchtocracy system of government, so, the problem of Africa is government by the leaders, for the people, by their godfathers, for democracy is government of the people, for the people by the people.

Nobody can solve the problem created by Africans better than Africans. President Barrack Obama made it clear to Africans in his speech on his visit to Ghana sometime in 2009, and I strongly believe that after the visit of the US president to Ghana African leaders would have a second thought, for second thoughts are often the best. It is very important to note that president Barrack Obama is an American president elected by the good people of America to protect the interest of America, and obviously not for Africa. African leaders should know that he is not an African president, because he was not elected into office by African countries, therefore, the president who took oath to work according to what is written in the American constitution will never leave the foreign policies of America to do something else, so, the president of the USA, Mr.

Barrack Obama can never feel for Africa beyond the feelings the people of America have for Africa. Though Obama may have his root in Africa through paternal genealogy which made him an African by birth, he is an American by citizenship, therefore, he is no more an African, perhaps it may interest you to know that when he gets old and dies he will never be buried in Africa, for no president in the history of this world has been buried outside the country that elected him a leader. Therefore, Africans should expect what they expected from George Bush, Bill Clinton and a host of others from Barrack Obama, because he is an American president, elected in clear voting system of democracy not by selection. Other presidents that have ruled America in the past have their root somewhere, therefore, Barrack Obama will not be an exemption. He can only help Africa to set up a formidable democratically elected government that will be operational if Africans want to help themselves, after all, a lot of American presidents in the past have at one time or the other tried to help Africa, but Africans were not ready, let us see if they will listen to Obama.

CHAPTER THREE

TRUE DEMOCRACY

What is true democracy? It is a political setting based on voting system of choosing leaders. It is a system that allows every citizen to exercise his rights by voting and be voted for. It is also a system that allows the people of a state or country to chose who rules them. In a country that operates a true democracy true federalism is visible. True democracy and good government will prosper where there is true federalism, but in a situation where people are living in pretentious system of government, bad government will be in place, because wrong people will always be chosen to represent the people, from the local to the state and to the federal level. Such system will pave way for misrepresentation of the people, and a system of government where people are misrepresented, embezzlement and mismanagement of public fund will be in place. In most countries where these systems of politics are mismanaged it will pave way for things like:

- Corruption
- Tribalism
- Marginalization
- Creation of many useless ministries to get more confused people in government.
- Implementation of useless programmes at the expense of the good ones.
- Setting up of deceitful panels to deceive people.
- Endless political crisis.
- Lack of people oriented programmes
- Breakdown of law and order
- Lack of good infrastructure
- Electoral malpractices
- Appointment by compromise, not by merit
- Political killings
- Massive unemployment
- Poor standard of living
- Disorganized system of education
- Lack of good healthcare delivery
- Underpayment of workers mostly teachers and retirees
- Lack of good roads
- Subjection of professionals to suffering in the interest of quacks

These and many others are what you see in a country where system of politics is bad and deceitful. Bad and deceit have the same character but are quite different in action. Something can be very bad but not deceitful, or deceitful but not bad. One can be very bad due to the character such individual has, someone may be doing wrong things but may not be deceitful, but if such a person can listen to corrections he might turn over a new leaf. A bad person is always direct in action, very straight in movement and will always oppose advice, hence it is very easy to avoid a bad person than a deceitful person. A deceitful person knows what is right, but will try as much as he can to deceive people about it. Even if anybody tries to advice such individual he will pretend to have accepted such advice. Deceitful people go to people as friends just to have their way that is why in a country where there is democracy, but not true democracy, the leaders are no doubt very deceitful.

In this topic we shall consider it in three subtopics with what I call democratic table to make my points comprehensive.

1. The merit and demerit of true democracy.
2. The merit and demerit of true federalism.
3. The reconciliation of merit and demerit of both true democracy and true federalism.

MERIT AND DEMERIT OF TRUE DEMOCRACY

We shall first consider the merit of true democracy. In a democratic setting with good structure, the system of governance should be government of the people, by the people and for the people. Such system will definitely produce government of the people. In a country where true democracy is in place, people have right to decide who leads them, with their votes. Anybody that is coming to lead the people should have the interest of the people at heart. In a country where true democracy is functional godfathers will be out of business, because politics will be seen as gambling, which means it is a game of winner takes all and looser goes home as a sports man. It is going to be a meeting of people that are for national interest, meaning that personal interest will have to die. In a true democratic system, patriotism will be the order of the day, true democracy is all about true patriotism, as such, democrats are allowed to play the game hence it is a game of sportsmanship. And where true patriots are fronted and genuinely elected as leaders, the people go home to sleep, because their interest will be well protected. For an individual to cast his or her vote for someone shows that such a person is trustworthy, so, people can candidly vouch their nobility and such individual must be capable to protect general interest. In a true democracy, national interest subdues personal interest. True democracy paves way for developments, because everybody will make contributions in whatever way they are capacitated, all in an effort to enhance national and human development.

True democracy paves way for political stability and the structures laid down should be for the people's interest not for personal enrichment. True democracy does not allow tribalism, corruption, marginalization and insecurity, for the laid-down structure will take care of every facet of national empowerment and development.

Looking at the merit of true democracy one will conclude that Nigeria and other African countries have failed, because the laid-down structures of democracy are nothing to write home about. A country that says they are operating under the platform of true democracy, but cannot boast of one credible election is a joker. A country that has a democratic institution that is stage-managed by some powerful individuals in power cannot get anything right in all facet of life. This is because the democratic setting is wrong and as such, such government is wrongly placed locally and internationally, for such democratic institution will only produce wrong people that will form wrong government that does not have the interest of the people at heart.

When we have true democracy in Africa it will not allow dubious power brokers to have their way in the corridors of power, and godfatherism system of democracy. It will not allow election by selection, nor pave way for 'do or die' politicking. It will not allow hired killers to remain in business, neither tribalism and marginalization nor the executive to control other arms of government at will. It will not allow bribery and corruption, it means that self enrichment will become a thing of the past. It will not allow non-implementation of budget, winning election at all cost will be jointly fought to a standstill. People that want to be in government either by hook or crook will not be told before they willingly step aside, because all what they are tirelessly gunning for in the corridor of power will no longer be within their reach. So, true democracy is too expensive, for a country to operate true democracy it means that the leaders will be sincere to the core.

DEMERITS OF TRUE DEMOCRACY

Demerit of true democracy means political mismanagement, because it is a total torture for the people. It is a situation where everybody in the society is subjected to the rule of law. It is so, because the brunt of conflicts, power tussle, political killings, election malpractices which are happening everywhere in the world is usually borne by the poor. Wherever, and whenever there is political crisis, it hits hard on the poor. When political leaders loot the treasury, the poor suffer unjustly. In a country where there is political instability the poor suffer it all, everything that can be beneficial to the poor will be totally denied.

Today in Nigeria, the people in power have succeeded in crippling the educational system thereby making it impossible for people from poor background to have quality education. Children of the rich are either overseas schooling or in the big private schools built by their fathers or relatives, while some rich people who have not built their own universities do send their children to the most expensive private universities operating in the country which are not within the reach of the poor. Public primary and secondary schools have been abandoned for the children of the poor. Reason is that, the government has grounded public schools so that those who want their children to go to school should look for how to steal or get involved in one crime or the other in order to afford school fees for their children.

It is on record that several Nigerians often go to bed without food. There are no good roads, let alone good water, but the rich enjoy things at will. There was a new government slogan sometime ago which says 'education for all by the year 2015, electricity for all by the year 2010 and housing for all by the year 2020', and many more. But all of these are becoming 'TV money.' TV money means money spent on TV only with no practical evidence on ground. This is what people call TV money. This is why all the roads in the federation are constructed with billions of naira still no good road anywhere. Government has invested billions in the energy sector, yet, the country is living in total blackout. Billions of naira invested in water sector, yet, no water supply for the people. All these billions of naira and dollars we hear without seeing the impact is 'TV money'.

General Yakubu Gowon was in power when I was born. From Gowon's government power was transferred to Gen Murtala Mohamed, Gen Obasanjo, Alhaji Shagari, Gen Buhari, Gen Babangida, Gen Abacha, Chief Ernest Shonekan, Gen Abubakar, Rtd Gen Olusegun Obasonjo to Late Alhaji Musa

Yar' Adua and from Dr Goodluck Jonathan to the present man in power Dr Goodluck E. Jonathan, it has been introduction of one policy or the other that will always keep the people of Nigeria in high spirit of expectations. One can only say that the government of Gen Murtala Mohamed would have been a new dawn in Nigeria, but that pregnancy was aborted by the bullets of Col Dinka which made Gen Obasanjo to take over power, and handed over to civilian government, and that is what his government will be remembered for. Gen Gowon's government was full of hydra-headed troubles, but after the war, what next? The elders will tell better stories of the regime that provoked Gen Murtala's coup.

Now looking at all these governments with their different policies, one will expect that by now Nigeria would have been getting it right at least, but instead of making cogent improvement people are being fooled the more by politicians. The summary is that, Nigerians are suffering and all Africans are crying, because when Nigeria is in trouble all Africans, home and abroad, will be affected in one way or the other. In a democracy, vote of the people brings government to their door step, because it counts. In Nigeria and some other African countries, people's vote brings hunger, suffering and human rights abuse. In a country where democracy is well structured, people will always be happy with the government, because life will be easy and one will not hear things like: political zone, you are not an indigene of this state, etc, therefore, you cannot. In Africa, if your father and mother are not from a place it does not matter how many years you have been in such place, the individual if not an indigenous person cannot stand for any elective position in such place, if such a person tries to make use of his citizenship he'll be killed overnight. In a country where democratic structures are very bad there will be total breakdown of law and order. People who have money will block all the route of opportunities against the poor. People will be subjected to social vices, even animals will not be exempted. The table below displays the merits and demerits of true democracy.

MERITS		DEMERITS
Good governance	1	Politicians will not have much money
Credible elections	2	Many people will have access to power
True federalism	3	The Rich will be subjected to rule of law
Infrastructural development	4	The executive powers will be limited
Political stability	5	government will be under serious checks and balances
Good healthcare delivery	6	Election will be by voting not by selection
Good educational system	7	Nobody will acquire government properties without accounting for it

Functional security system	8	People will work hard to earn a living
Steady power supply	9	Indigenes can lose elective position
Protection of human right	10	Many rich people may end up in prisons
Appointments by merit	11	Everybody will be totally caged by law
Good roads and water supply	12	The rich can lose their respect
Housing facilities for all	13	Politicians will be facing much challenges at polls
No tribalism	14	Money will no longer decide who wins election
National interest first	15	People's hope will be expanded
Respect for rule of law	16	Nobody will claim ownership of land
Respect for arms of government	17	The legislature will not make much money
End of political zones	18	Legislative arm of government will be part time
End of economy looting	19	Some political benefits will stop
Rapid growth of economy	20	Political criminals will be out of business

THE MERITS AND DEMERITS OF TRUE FEDERALISM

A country where true federal system of government is in place, democracy is always free from internal problems. People will not have much interest vested on the federal government, but will be interested in the state, because every state will be autonomous. The federal government will have limited power in the state, the executives of the state are responsible for state affairs. That is why states in a country under true federalism do have things like:

- State police
- State laws
- State policy
- Resource control
- State electoral system
- State security system
- State power generating policy
- State taxation policy
- State social services policy
- State labour policy
- State developmental policy, etc.

This means that each state under true federalism is more like a country on its own, because they will be allowed to have control over everything under the central law of the country. It is important to note that true federalism gives the states more internal powers to control, manage and hold on their own. It is not that the states are not being guided by the federal laws, it is just that each state under the true federalism does the business of the state not the federal government. This is the type of democracy that exists in civilized world like the USA. Africans are emulating the American democracy, but they have refused to abide by the policies and principles of true democracy that is why they are not getting things right in terms of:

- Electoral process
- Democratic management of rights
- Human management
- Respect for rule of law
- Resource control
- Internal and external securities
- The rights of states and that of the federation
- Interpretation of central policies and democratic policies
- Pure interpretation of separation of power
- Pure interpretation of private sector, states and the federal government commitment in business and development of infrastructures under true federalism
- Pure interpretation of private sector, states and federal government commitment in the provision of social and essential amenities under true federalism.

All that is enlisted above are the areas the African governments are doing little or nothing to properly correct, because if all these are well interpreted it means that democracy is working. But owing to inadequate/poor interpretation of these issues, Africans will continue to fight one another over:

- Resource control
- Marginalization and tribalism
- None provision of social and essential amenities for the people
- No respect for judiciary
- The executive control of other arms of government.
- Bad electoral process
- Abuses on the rights of people
- Recycling of people in power
- Corruption at higher increase
- Insecurity, etc.

In Africa, we don't have true democracy and the leaders are not ready to operate under such platform. Africans are in love with monopoly system of governance, which is a system where the federal executive decides what happens in a country without due consultation. It is a situation where the state executives are the house boys of the federal executives. It is a situation where laws are made for the poor not for the powerful. A situation where politics is for personal enrichment. A situation where government is for the few privileged ones, not for the general public. What a system!There are two types of democracy__ direct and indirect. Indirect democracy is what is practiced in modern world (including the U.S.A), unlike direct democracy which was practiced in ancient Greece. Africa is the place where the president becomes all in all, hence, fighting and crying of the people can never stop until the right step is taken in the right direction. Politics is for personal enrichment in Africa, this prompted the people of a particular state in Nigeria to present a candidate from almost every family vying for the office of a governor. What should one expect in such a place?

There is serious money in Nigerian politics, and indeed some other African countries too, once you are in government of the day, you are an already-made billionaire. People bribe their way into government, then, what do you think that such a person will do first? The individual will first of all recoup his investment with enough interest/profit then, the need and want of his godfathers will be met with, as all the godfathers will bring their own choice of persons for official appointments into various offices. Oh what a system! Nigeria is a very big business for self acclaimed politicians.

True federalism is considered the opium of true democracy, while true democracy is the anchor of a well structured political system. It is one that paves way for another in the building of a stable development of an electoral process so as to have a better leadership in a country. The table below displays the merits and demerits of true federalism.

MERITS		DEMERIT
States will have more power	1	Federal government lose some powers to the states
There will be lesser political crisis	2	The executives both federal and states will not be authoritative
Government will get closer to the people	3	Indigenes will lose their indigenous rights
States will take care of security as they like	4	The electorates will have power over their votes
Federal government will have lesser problems	5	Non indigenes will have access to government
Government will be for people who want to serve	6	Government will not have total control of mineral resources
Electoral system will be better, for states will decide what happens in their states	7	It is more expensive to maintain true federalism

THE RECONCILIATION OF MERIT AND DEMERIT OF TRUE DEMOCRACY AND TRUE FEDERALISM

In politics, there are different ways of achieving goals or getting results, that is why the world directly or indirectly is witnessing different kinds of politics and its activities. In all systems of politics that exist there are popular ones that people recognize or are more familiar with.

1. Democracy
2. Monarchical system of governance

The world is much familiar with these two systems of politics leaving behind other systems which some countries are using to 'appoint' their leaders.

-   Militocracy
-   Thugritocracy
-   Autocracy
-   Replacementocracy
-   Familiatocracy
-   Zonitocracy
-   Windowcracy

These are systems of politics in the world that are not usually included in any country's constitution. None of these systems of politics are recognized by any country, hence, people do get worried whenever any of these is demonstrated. These systems of politics are functional in the third world countries, mostly Africa. Each of the system in place has its own character and way of approach, that is why it is a system. Almost all of these systems have been used by Nigerians alone, yet, we are still not getting things right, because most of them have characteristics of democracy except one which is purely militarian.

I will be shading light on these systems of democracy, for the countries that have practiced them and those still practicing them.

MILITOCRACY

This is a situation where soldiers have left their duty post to take over government forcefully, breaking the rules and order of governance. In this kind of situation such government is considered illegal, because it does not operate constitutionally.

CHARACTERISTICS

Each time a country experience military coup, the political system of such country will be removed from the constitutional rule of law provided by the country's constitution to laws provided by the military ruling council which is outside the existing constitution. However, the difference between the two is, in the rule of law provided by the constitution, people go to court to get justice even against the government. Which means, a person can go to court and get justice to remove a sitting officer who was duly elected by the people, for example, a president, governor, etc. But in the law provided by military rule, people do go to court without getting justice, unless proven by the military head of government. Constitutional rule of law does not give any elected officer absolute power, hence, the head of government can be removed by means of law provided by the constitution, whereas in the military laws such is not possible. The military head is the alter ego of such government, unless another military coup comes up to topple the regime. Constitutional rule of law did not approve of a president or governor sacking a legislator who is duly elected, but a military head of state can sack a member of the military provisional ruling council, because nobody elected them, for it is the military head of government that appointed them.

About 98% of countries of Africa have experienced military rule, so it is difficult for one to start listing the countries that have and those that have not experienced it.

THUGRITOCRACY

This is another system of government mostly used by politicians, it is very popular in Africa. It is adopted by Nigerian politicians as bodyguards without knowing that it is a system of government. In politics, whichever means a person uses to achieve his political aims and objectives, such is a system. It could be dubious, or morally okay, but what matters is that politically something has happened to see someone through to the seat of power. When one says that there is a system, it means, a means of achieving something very important to that individual or to another person. It means a system can be legal or illegal if the constitution did not approve of it, or if it is not political. For example, an organization in charge of a situation in which an individual who is striving to formulate another system of making things happen but had in their constitution that a particular already existing system cannot be changed by anybody who disagrees with the individual while trying to introduce another system, then, such system becomes illegal, but if not otherwise proven, any system used by anybody to achieve aims and objectives remains legal.

THE ILLEGALITY OF THUGRITOCRACY

This is illegal because it is widely condemned by all countries of the world, it is an act of criminality. In Nigeria, all the politicians have their well trained thugs, ready at all times to fight and steal ballot boxes. They are masters in the area of harassing and killing of opposition members. This, no doubt, prompted the belief that political killings in Nigeria cannot stop. For better understanding of this claim, all the people killed in Nigeria and those that disappeared from the days of the military regime to date, government has not been able to bring anybody to book, except the former chief security officer of the then military head of state Gen Sani Abacha, the only assumed corrupt leader in Nigeria. One would wonder why this is so. The reason is that he is dead. If he had been alive, probably he would have become one of the most trusted leaders in the country's political history. No doubt, when a man dies, his ideas and opinions die with him, but if he is alive he can defend himself, this is how people are assumed to be corrupt in Nigeria.

Thugry as a word means a lot of things to people, because it has a character which is part of human life, that is why it can be framed as the negative character of a person that makes an individual negative among positive people. It can also be seen as irresponsible behaviour in a person that makes a person irresponsible among responsible individuals.

In a country where system of politics is practised, politics becomes a death trap. In a country where such system is the order of the day people with good intentions will not be in government. When people are pretending over everything it means that truth is totally dead. Thugritocracy is a system of politics that looks like democracy, but is far from it. It is pretentious, it is criminal, it is dubious, it is too harmful, it does not allow free and fair elections, it does not allow peace and justice, it does not allow harmony. Thugritocracy is a killer, it is an enemy of man, because it kicks against good governance, it encourages evil people to kill good people like goats without respect for humanity, God will help Africa!

REPLACEMENTOCRACY

This is a system that is usually possible in a mechanical environment. It is so because mechanical system of government is all about using someone to replace the deceased or retired leader, not by election. It could be either by selection or merit. In some cases when a person dies, the person's close relation will be asked to replace him. Apart from the officially known monarchical system which deals with the issue of replacement, if the son of the deceased did not replace his late father the closest relation will do, such system is not the character of democracy except on grounds of impeachment then any other person takes over to replace the impeached leader, but it must also be by merit.

In addition to that, replacementocracy can take place in a democratic system that is unhealthy. The following can make democracy unhealthy:—

- Criminals in politics
- Godfatherism
- Dubious intentions
- Corrupt system
- Non implementation of electoral laws
- Bad electoral policies
- Corrupt political structures
- Tribalism and marginalization

In a democratic structure where all these are in place the democratic system will be very bad, as such, anything can happen. Replacementocracy system of government is criminal, because it neither allow people with good intentions to be elected as leaders nor does it allow people's vote to count during elections. It does not allow justice to prevail over electoral matters. It causes developmental delay and does not encourage good governance. It does not allow protection of human rights, because its nature encourages human rights abuse. It encourages corruption from the low to high level of living, it does not allow protection of lives and properties, because its nature is crime. It encourages poverty in the nation. It allows the poor to get poorer and the rich richer. It kills economic power of a nation and gets the future destroyed. It ruins every move for youth empowerment. It destroys the educational sector. It discourages agricultural reforms. It puts a country in a state of insecurity, thereby scares away investors. Teachers would not be paid or under paid. Its web of corruption sinks energy sector. It encourages non implementation of the country's budget. It skyrockets joblessness due to ill programmes put up for job creation.

In a country where replacementocracy system of politics exists people with evil desires will always have their way to the seat of power, because they might have enriched themselves dubiously. They will therefore use their ill-gotten wealth and dubious political might to cause poverty among the people. Still, they come back to people pretending to be saints as they use the same wealth to bribe their way through and buy people's conscience to ensure their stay in power. When they see an opposition with good intentions they will make efforts to make such individual become part of their government. The reason is that, they want to ensure that such person's good intentions are totally destroyed. In some African countries this kind of democracy is functioning directly and indirectly. Some of these countries are:

- Congo DR
- Gabon
- Nigeria
- Togo, etc.

In Nigeria replacementocracy is in operation, because it is a country where politics of special interest that is based on greed is operational. In Nigeria, replacementocracy is the game, this is why leaders who smuggled themselves into the seat of power shop for those that would replace them at the expiration of their tenure so that all their evil deeds will be covered, that means, people's votes would not count.

In Congo DR, Togo and Gabon direct replacementocracy is the game. Due to the high level of corruption in Nigeria the leaders are always afraid during campaign and election period, because they do not know what the future holds for them if they allow free and fair election. This is the reason Nigeria runs a system considered as 'multi-political one-party system of democracy'. There are lots of political parties, yet, it is one party that is all-in-all, because it is practically impossible for another political party to defeat the ruling party. One can come into power through a political party during election, thereafter, such can dump such party for the ruling party for continuity, else, they will lose the next election.

The democratic republic of Congo is a country that was eaten up by corruption for so many years. The country suffered a lot of setbacks in the regime of late Mobutu, a country that had a president who was considered to be richer than the entire nation. It was at the height of misgovernance of the country by Mobutu's corrupt leadership that Mr. Kabila rebelled and seized power. When Kabila declared war on Mobutu he could not trust many people and many did not trust him as well, because every opinion in the country was based on personal interest. Though he succeeded by seizing power, but he could not achieve much before he was corruptly killed. His death was technically masterminded from his camp. The consequence of his death then paved way for his son to come into the picture, but it is understandable that corruption in a country paves way for rebellion, and from rebellion to civil leadership, because nobody could be trusted anymore, everybody will become a suspect.

Togo and Gabon have no reason for their actions, because the fathers of these new breed of leadership were not the best in these countries. And there was no much achievement made over the years that could form stronghold of their positions, rather, it was corruption all the way. The implication would be the continuation of corruption and intimidation of oppositions in both countries. Africa should get up and look into their actions and consider their ways over matters, because a little child will not continue to be a boy after several years. In the U.S.A George Bush (senior) was once a president, he lost his seat to Bill Clinton in his second term bid. Some years later his son came back and won election in a clearer manner, because Mr. Al-Gore did not go to court to challenge that election. It was alleged that voting was free and fair like all elections in America, although the counting of votes was done overtime because people of America wanted to be sure of what they were doing. Bush's regime was unpopular in America, yet, it was the same regime that conducted the best elections so far in the history of the States and handed over power to the first African-American (black) president. Mr. Bush was clean during and after the elections. It has gone down in history that it was his government that conducted elections that ushered in the first black president in America, putting aside one of the world's deadliest viruses (racism) of the time. If anybody in Africa desire the office of his father dead or living, let it not be through 'replacementocracy system', the seat of power is nobody's private business. If it were in Africa George Bush would not have handed over to an opposition, instead he would have looked for a replacement by himself.

AUTOCRACY

Autocracy is autocratic system of government, it is a system that gives the head of government absolute power. Autocracy is not a democratic system of government, it is a system that is very common with the military. A lot of African countries have suffered setbacks from the military at one time or the other. There is no African nation without such experience this is why democratic structures in most African countries are filled with corruption making development in Africa impossible. Young army officers who are looking for self enrichment will seize power from civilians in the guise that politicians are corrupt, hence, they will come and start seeking foreign support, worse still, they will promise them all kinds of things, making them see reason why they should support them against civilians. This system is one of the weapon that destroyed Africa's politics, all the people that supported coups in Africa are the same condemning Africans and even banning Africans from entering their countries. They believe Africans are very corrupt. I have respect for American government for their fight against autocratic rule in our world today, no doubt such fight is beginning to pave way for better things to come, but foreign nations that supported military rule in Africa, especially in Nigeria should please release to Africa all the stolen money banked or invested in one dubious business or the other in their countries, because if they allow such wealth to still remain with them, they should know that they are more corrupt than corrupt African leaders. If they are able to return the money to the countries where it was taken from, with the help of God and other good friends of Africa surely Africa will begin to experience good democracy not autocracy, then, the people of Africa will sing the song of development.

Autocracy is an enemy of human right. Autocratic system of government is considered one man's government, its products are:

- Economy loot
- Bribery
- Human right abuses
- Bad governance
- Killings and destruction of properties
- Destruction of democratic structure
- High level of crime and injustice
- Hunger and poverty
- Embarrassment of oppositions
- Godfatherism, tribalism and marginalization

These and many others are the real characters of autocracy and when these are in place, such a system is considered an enemy of progress and national development.

FAMILIATOCRACY

This system of democracy is not known to people, but today, it is functioning all over the world. Familiatocracy is a system that is based on familiarism otherwise called 'Man-know-man' system of government.

It is a Man-know-man government of interest based on human connections, not according to the wish and interest of the people. It can be defined as a political system that is hijacked by some powerful individuals to enrich and get their relations, friends and close pals satisfied at the expense of the majority. Now, having said this, one will then understand that this system of government is very corrupt, it does not speak well of politics in a country, it does not make things easy for the common man. I have not seen where this kind of government succeeded and delivered the dividend of democracy to the people. Nigeria government from 1979 to date is a good example.

In 1979, Gen Olusegun Obasanjo handed over to Alhaji Shehu Shagari because it was said that the man who scored the highest number of votes did not win two third of the total votes cast, that was why a mathematician called Professor Chike Obi was called to help the government out over the matter. Dr. Azikiwe of NPP then added his votes to Shagari's to help him score the much needed two third and that was how the mathematics of Chike Obi saw the nation through. Majority of Nigerians did not know that the government of the day was not in Chief Awolowo becoming the president of Nigeria, because he might not agree to protect some dubious interest. Then I knew that there was an election, but I didn't know what brought the president into power because I was still underage. Nigerians have been denied their rights time without number. Why did the government not allow a run off election for the actual winner to emerge? Why would the government allow the overnight merger of the NPP and NPN? The answer is very simple, the government of the day did not want to see the face of Chief Awolowo coming to takeover power from them, because whoever the president is leaving the seat of power in Nigeria, such president must surely replace himself with a government he can still control from his house. So, in 1979 Awolowo was not familiar with the government of the day, therefore, he was considered not trustworthy to manage Nigeria. In 1993 another kind of democracy came on board, there was an election which was considered free and fair by observers all over the world, but the winner of that election chief MKO Abiola fell out of favour with the military junta, therefore, he was not to be trusted. So, NRC and SDP ended their journey after that election that refused to produce a president for Nigerians, eventually, all the political institutions were abolished. I do not want to mention the interim government headed by Chief Ernest Shonekan, because such was a military idea. He was used as a pawn However, in as much as the government that brought the interim government into power was unconstitutional, for such government legality was not recognized by the Nigerian constitution, such government cannot take legal action, therefore, as the government that introduced interim government was illegal, so was the interim government.

In 1999, everybody thought that Dr. Alex Ekwueme would become the president of Nigeria due to his popularity and contributions towards having a democratic institution in Nigeria. But because he was unlikely to protect the evil and atrocities committed by the present and past military heads of state, Gen Olusegun Obasanjo (rtd) was nominated to become the president, obviously by some power brokers in the country. As they gathered themselves in Abuja to give the former military head the ticket as their presidential candidate, a leader then made a statement saying that if Dr. Ekwueme was allowed to become the president he will go on exile. So, in 1999 Nigerians witnessed the first 'militocracy' based on 'familiatocracy'.

In the year 2007, 'replacementocracy' that is based on 'familiatocracy' took place which made the outgoing president to say that the election was going to be a 'do or die' affair. Today, all these are history and Nigerians are still suffering, they painfully bear the brunt. It is only in Nigeria that a leader will leave his office to go and campaign for the person who will replace him. Nigerians, let us tell ourselves the simple truth about us, nobody can tell the truth better on the journey so far than us.

ZONITOCRACY

Zonitocracy is a system of government that is allowed in a country where there is diverse tribal groups. In a multi-ethnic nation there is bound to be different kinds of characters, interest and opinions over political matters. Situation like this is likely to occur in a country where people are forced to come together or in a country that has disagreement over their constitution, which before hand did not properly spell out how the people should be governed. In a country where people have written policies and principles you do not expect total peace, because there is going to be tribal sentiments, -marginalization. The reason is that such country does not operate constitutionally, but in principles and policies, as such, the system of governance must pave way for crisis. A particular ethnic group that has a large number of people and landmark is bound to have much states, much local councils, much development, because it is the number of states and local council in a place that brings the governmental development to the common man in various villages.

In a constitution that is well accepted by all and sundry, the interest of big and small ethnic groups will be protected making it very possible for people to see reason why they should belong to such country. But in policies and principles the small and smaller ethnic groups are not protected, because the clauses in the written document only protect the larger interest group leaving the opinions of the smaller ones to suffer cruel neglect.

The smaller groups will not produce enough states not even local council like the larger ethnic groups that will give them the required votes that can form a government.

What is written policies and principles? This is a document written by associations, group of people that want to form a government. It is like a constitution, it is very close to it, because it has articles that give some people power to govern, power to make laws, power to enforce laws and power to prosecute offenders of the law. It has power that gives people right to live and to some extent protects people's rights, power to go to court, power to vote and be voted for, but it lacks what I call unification power that gives people the sense of belonging. For example:

- True federalism
- True democracy
- Protection of smaller ethnic groups' rights
- Sharing of power by the big and smaller ethnic groups
- Landmarks rights
- Power for resource control
- Grassroots development policy that accommodates all ethnic groups

These and many more are the articles that are missing in the written document called principles and policies. It isn't that they are not there, sometimes they are clearly written, but the problem however is that it lacks implementation force. It lacks such because the document was not written by the people, but by few interest groups that gathered themselves somewhere to decide how the people will be governed.

What is a constitution? It can be defined as a collection of norms or standards according to which a country is governed. It contains statements intended to define the relations between rulers and the ruled, the basic institutional framework of government, the rights and duties of the citizens and many important procedures to be followed. The constitution defines the atmosphere for the practice of legitimate power; who shall execute political powers, how they shall execute it and their limitations. It may be a vague body of unwritten laws taking the form of usages, understanding, customs or conventions which are not recognized as laws, but are not less effective in controlling the government, as in Britain.

More so, it can be a detailed written document as in the United States of America, Nigeria, etc, In these states the constitution is a carefully prepared and organized written document in which the organization of the government, the powers and its relations to individuals are carefully set down. Further more, a constitution may be said to be a document which contains the principles upon which the government is founded and regulated. As previously stated it is classified into written and unwritten constitution. A constitution can be rigid or flexible. Unwritten constitution is often being regarded as the flexible one, while the rigid is referred to as the written constitution. It is regarded as rigid because it is more fundamental, they apply to more general and significant matters than the ordinary law. Its laws are not easily changed, its rate of change is slower than that of changes in the ordinary or flexible law. It has a legal binding, whenever it wants to be changed it is done through judicial review. Written constitutions are regarded as supreme law, for it requires some lengthy or difficult process to alter. The usual processes of amendment provided through the initiative of the legislature alone, by the convention of conventions created for the purpose and by the popular vote through the initiative referendum. Rigid constitution varies considerably both in the methods provided for amending them and, in the extent of difficulty they experience in adjusting themselves to changing situation. On the other hand, a flexible constitution is the one which can be changed without lengthy or difficult process.

Looking at the definitions of both written and unwritten documents you will clearly understand that the constitution clearly spell out the behaviour of the ruler and the ruled, the possibles and impossibles of both party. In the written constitution the rulers and the ruled act and behave within the provisions of law making it impossible for anybody to live above the law. Written principles and policies share almost the same features, but it is flexible because the clauses in it can be altered by anybody in authority.

Now in 'zonitocracy', the issue of clauses in the written constitution is not in play, because a written constitution which contains the opinion and ideas of the generality of people cannot be changed overnight just to accommodate the zoning system of the government, bear in mind that zoning system of government is not a democratic system. It is based on selection of people from various zones to manage the affairs of people. Sometimes those chosen from these zones might not be the right people to deliver the dividend of democracy to the people. Zonitocracy does not give room for political fair play and it is baseless, it does not give equity and justice. There is no government in this world that does not have system and constitution, call it flexible or rigid, there must be a system and there must be a constitution, because the rulers and the ruled must know their responsibilities. Why does a country like Nigeria operate zonitocracy system of government? There is a written document in place called constitution, but it lacks the opinion of the people. People of Nigeria have been governed by different kinds of leaders beginning from the colonial days to the days of indigenous government.

In 1960 it was the document handed over by the colonial masters to the people of Nigeria which was amended overtime in the name of writing a constitution for the country. When the military took over government those papers were sidelined, because no military operates constitutionally, except laws they put in place to favour their unconstitutional regime. As they continued in power they continued to make laws for the people of Nigeria until 1979 when they wanted to hand over government to civilians, they came together to write what is called 1979 constitution that introduced the civilian government headed by Alhaji Shehu Shagari. Overtime, this constitution written by the soldiers has been amended without yielding any good fruit. During the days of the military President of Nigeria, Gen Ibrahim Babangida, he set up what was called national constitutional conference to look into the Nigeria constitution, but all to no avail. Till date, Nigerian people do not have a constitution that contains the opinions and ideas of Nigerians, that is why ethnic groups in the country are not at home with one other. The people have not come together to discuss and agree in principles and policies, and then write a constitution on how they should be governed. The people have not come together to discuss how they should co-exist as one people and one nation. This is the reason why some powerful men are superior to the constitution, the rulers and the ruled are not working together. The interest of Nigeria is not in anybody's heart, but all the ethnic groups in the country are complaining about one thing or the other:—

- No equity in state creation
- No equity in job creation
- No equity in electoral reforms
- No equity in the recruitment of military and the police force.
- No equity in political appointments
- No equity in power sharing
- No equity in resource control

- No equity in the judiciary
- No equity in citizens' rights

Nigeria as a country has applied a lot of political options just to silence the tribalized and marginalized, but Nigerians are not happy, because the system is very bad. Now we are in the zoning system, a new option discovered in 1999 which brought in the retired army general from south-west into power, he stayed in office for eight years, then it was the turn of Alhaji Yar'Adua from north-west, which means the north will control power for eight years. The system allows the six geo-political zones we have in Nigeria to take their slot in the presidency. Any constitutional amendment that does not allow the remaining four zones to have their own eight years at the presidency will cause serious problems in the country. Nigeria is one of the countries that operate zonitocracy system of government, because everything has gone wrong from the beginning. It will only be corrected if God help to raise a wise democrat from other zones into power to effect changes in the Nigerian politics.

WINDOWCRACY

'Windowcracy' system of politics is criminal, because it does not present politics as it should be. It does not protect the electorate and it is a bad image for democracy. Its character is to get into power either by hook or crook. Windowcracy is the most deadly option in politics, it makes politics uninteresting and stupid. This is a system that rubbishes all other options, it shows how incompetent a country is in the business of politics and organizing elections. Almost all the countries of this world have at one time or the other taken part in windowcracy politics. Till date, Africans are still practicing it openly, while in some western countries it has been indirect with such option, because it is an old fashioned system of politics.

Windowcracy is no more fashionable, because it is an option most valued by political criminals who want to win elections at all costs, even when they are rejected by the people they want to rule. Windowcracy is welcomed and valued in a country where citizens have lost their conscience, it makes things easier for electoral criminals and worsen the conditions of the real democrats.

What is windowcracy? It can be defined as a suitable criminal option of politics made possible by criminal politicians. This is used in every election to ensure a successful rigging of elections and defrauding of electoral acts. It can be seen as a system of politics that has its character anchored on crime and pretence. The reason it is so is that, it has its bedrock in criminality.

a. Every character of windowcracy does not mean well for humanity, therefore it is criminal for a nation to get involved in it.

b. It is pretentious. It presents itself to the public as a saint, is inherently deceitful.
c. It takes life that it cannot replace at will and jeopardizes people's chances of good governance.
d. It causes backwardness to a nation and puts a country behind others in terms of infrastructural development.
e. It makes incompetent people to be in government and it encourages practical killing and abuse of human rights.

These are the reasons why windowcracy is evil and cannot be allowed to function in a nation. A study of the world's system of politics will reveal that most nations are using the option of windowcracy directly or indirectly. Windowcracy is not only visible during elections, it is also visible during party primaries, because those that will contest general elections are the people chosen by their political parties. Sometimes, during party primaries the opinion of the majority does not count due to this option. For example, the Nigeria party primaries.

In 1999, this option was adopted by PDP and ANPP primaries respectively, the powerful members of the parties produced Rtd. Gen Olusegun Obasanjo as PDP flag bearer and Rtd. Gen Mohamadu Buhari for ANPP. PDP adopted this option just to edge out the most likely contender Dr. Alex Ekwueme, that is why during the internal crisis of the PDP a state governor from south-east who accused the president of been corrupt alleged that the president was made a president in his house. What a shame! Presidents are being made in people's houses, no more by voting. Later on in his (Obasanjo) tenure the EFCC (Economic and Financial Crimes Commission) hunted the young governor, obviously for telling the nation about what transpired in 1999. He and some other governors were corrupt. They opposed the president's attempt to become president for life through third term, and probably fourth term, which is unconstitutional. All the people that did not support the third term bid were indeed very corrupt.

The ANPP used the windowcracy option openly in 1999 when they compelled all the presidential aspirants of the party to withdraw for a retired army general, because they believed they could outplay PDP aspirants since the two contenders of the number one seat in Nigeria were former army chiefs, but unknown to them election had since been concluded in someone's house, even before the primaries took place. On the night of the ANPP primaries, many felt regret and anger in the voice of the most successful politician, he came with the intention that there was going to be party primaries, only for the young man who invested so much money to see that the party stands the test of time, but to his dismay the primaries had been conducted before his arrival, consequently, he was asked to support the anointed candidate of the party, hence, humbled by circumstance. He thereafter decamped from ANPP to PDP. What a political system in Nigeria. I

In 2006 PDP primaries that produced the present people in power, we saw the adoption of windowcracy, because the most popular contender withdrew on the eve of the primaries. The question is, are there no likes of Barrack Obamas in Nigeria? Nigeria has millions of Obamas, but they won't dare declare their interest or good intentions because of the dirtiness of the Nigerian politics. It pains deeply beyond human imaginations, it takes God in such life to survive. I need not mention men and women of good intents, that have lost their lives due to Nigerian politics. It is agonizing pain to hear how virtues, talents are hunted to death, by some acclaimed spook.

CHAPTER FOUR

VISION AND UNDERSTANDING

The vision and understanding of leadership is what makes a leader outstanding, because the vision of a person is what people build upon to get a better future.

VISION OF A LEADER

Leadership is all about vision not ambition. A person can be very ambitious, yet, lacks vision which is the real thing. Vision is a directive for a leader, it makes a leader focused and directional. A leader that has sound vision cannot be dubious. He will not be personal. Every leadership vision is always for all. It is for all in the sense that people will not ask for directives before realizing such vision, as realizing a vision cannot be outside such vision. Every vision comes with a solution. Vision gets people born into the compound of ideas, it places things in their rightful position. It avoids confusion and distraction.

What is vision? Vision can be defined as a view of unseen events which puts an individual ahead of others. Vision can also be seen as strength to direct. It programmes ones future in a right direction for a better living.

Looking at the definitions of vision you will discover that the vision of a man is purely the man. A man of vision is never comfortable with his vision unrealized. A man of vision cannot be at home when he is not seeing proofs of his vision. Every leader conceives a vision for the people. It is the vision a leader has for the people that will make him a good leader.

A true leader can never be personal, he is passionate about his people and considers their interest first before any other thing. A leader leads to please and satisfy the needs of his people. A leader leads to make a mark and put himself in the minds of the people he is leading. A leader tolerates people and receives both insults and respect. A sincere leader leads by good examples. A pure leader is a pace setter. A leader cries and mourns whenever he loses one of his subjects. A true leader would prefer to be hungry to satisfy his people. A true leader cares for his people than himself and his family. A true leader is a father for all, he does not discriminate. A true leader is a counselor and people's solicitor and advocate of justice. A true leader feels the pains of others more than they do. A true leader is a watchman that watches over his people. A true leader believes in peace and dialogue to resolve issues. A leader is not autocratic. A true leader is always mindful of his actions even when things are not working out well to avoid discouraging his people. A true leader is only happy when the people are happy and gets frustrated when the people are not happy with him. People who are reasonable enough to know that they are not qualified leaders resign their appointment when the people are not working with their visions. The vision of a leader must anchor on leading and serving the people, not leading for the purpose of achieving selfish interest.

UNDERSTANDING OF LEADERSHIP POSITION

When a leader understands that leadership is not for self enrichment such leader will be willing to serve people who voted him into the position of leadership. It is the level of understanding of a leader that makes him successful and overcome all leadership challenges posed by a situation.

What is understanding?

Oxford dictionary defines understanding as knowing about a particular subject or situation. Understanding can also be defined as having general overview of all matters, subjects, situations, etc. It can as well be seen as a person being able to know all things set before him without trying to inquire from anybody. For example, Paul is a man of deeper understanding concerning our country's day to day activities. Therefore, for a person to have understanding means that such a person has wisdom, which means that understanding and wisdom are what brings vision into fulfillment. Without understanding and wisdom vision will not be in place, and without both as well one cannot realize his vision, because whatever anybody calls vision will be considered an illusion. Anyone that has understanding of his vision must realize it. Understanding opens the eyes of a wise man to see the vision and plan ahead of time. This will be better harnessed if grouped and discuss accordingly.

1. knowing what leadership is
2. What Africa should expect from Obama
3. Speedy fight against human rights abuses
4. My vision for Africa
5. My message to African friends

KNOWING WHAT LEADERSHIP IS

In our world of today many people are dreaming of becoming leaders without knowing what leadership is all about. One thing is to have leadership ambition, but the most important of it all is to have the vision of a leader. One can become a leader in the real sense, but the most crucial is to have leadership qualities. Aspiring to become is like desiring to become, while desiring to become is like dreaming to become, all these are according to an individual's mindset, they are not part of vision. Leadership qualities are far from just having a dream or desire, leadership qualities are far beyond ambition, because in leadership a lot of things are required and a lot of things are to be dealt with in order to have a competent leader. One does not just wake up one day to become a leader, leadership is not what one thinks or feels he can jump into. It is all about desiring to meet the needs of people and doing every reasonable thing to ensure that people's interest are well protected. It is the people that come first before a leader, one cannot put himself first as a leader before people and eventually have a feather added to his cap. Before tabulating leadership pre-requisites and the things that are to be dealt with if one wants to be a leader by example, let us first make effort to know and understand the true meaning of leadership.

Leadership means a lot to different people, this is why it has been widely misinterpreted by many aspiring leaders. To many people, leadership is merely becoming the head of a community or chairman of an organization, or perhaps becoming the president of a nation just to attract respect and make names for themselves. Though leadership positions are seen as the head, but leadership is simple, it is a call to serve, save, protect, inspire, encourage and work with the people. A leader is called to serve the people not to be served. The people come first before the leader. A leader is to serve by defending the people he leads from every external and internal aggression. A leader protects his people. A leader must be an inspiring person, he must be very creative and hard working, he must be able to make people see the future from their now. Every leader is a director of people's opinion. Leaders lead and direct people's affairs and opinions to get the best out of them. A leader is a counselor who encourages people to get the best out of them. A leader listens to his people in order to know how to counsel them for a better future. A good leader works with the people he is leading to get good result for the people.

Having considered these issues above as the qualities of a leader, it is obvious that good leaders live for the people and die for the people. To live and die for the people does not mean a leader should kill himself for the people, it means a leader does not live for himself alone to satisfy himself, he can only be satisfied when the people are happy.

As regards the requirements of a leader and the things to deal with, consider the items listed below.

REQUIREMENT	THINGS TO BE DEALT WITH
Truth	Lies
Listening ears	Carelessness
Open heartedness	Self-centeredness
Wisdom	Foolishness
Understanding	Boasting/pride

Knowledge	Ignorance
Open policy	Rigidity
Love and Care	Wickedness
Accountability	Criminality
Inspiration	Discouragement
Cleanliness	Dirtiness
Achievements	Laziness
Meekness	Anger
Wise speaker	Provocation
Great thinker	Jokes
Good intentions	Evil intentions
A visioner	Sleeping all the time
Content	Greediness
Comfortable	Covetousness
Hard work	Scorn

When you take critical look at these requirements of a leader and things to be dealt with, you will discover that our world is going through hard times, most leaders lack vital leadership qualities, most leaders do not know what it takes to be leaders. They do not understand the qualities required of leaders, they don't know how to vehemently deal with what is hidden in their lives. In Africa, some people think that one becomes a leader when such a person has so much money, or when a person is able to acquire university certificates. This is the sole reason people do all sort of dubious things to acquire money.

Terminating lives does not matter anymore, what matters is that one has made a lot of money to bribe his way through. Upon looting government treasury, they will enroll in one university either home or abroad and come out the next day with a PhD without merit. The only proof is that he had at one time or the other registered with one university and came out when the real students were leaving school. With such acquisition the individual is now qualified to be called a leader or be voted for as one. This is not the requirement for leadership. Money cannot buy the qualities of a leader and certificate cannot give the requirements of a leader.

When we discuss money and leadership, indeed money is needed to make some things happen all right, but money is not a character of a leader. Anybody can bring it from anywhere to establish a leader. When reasonable people who have money discover the qualities of leadership in a person they will not hesitate to bring out money to make the dream of such a person a reality. Knowledge is power, but this is not equally going to school and coming out without knowing what the person has gone to study. It entails going to school, studying what you know you are good at adding some to your divine leadership qualities, then, you can proudly and honestly say you are a sound leader. But a situation where a person who would have been better as a medical doctor is now studying political science just because he wants to be heard, or a lawyer, acting like a medical doctor, the situation will be very critical. Everybody cannot be a leader, because God did not create us the same, leaders are born.

Africans need good leaders not some dubious rich men who can afford to buy the seat of power dubiously to enrich themselves the more. Africans want men who have the interest of Africans at heart, not those who can buy themselves the seat of power and become what they desire, not those that visionalize just to steal. Africans are crying for good leaders.

WHAT AFRICA SHOULD EXPECT FROM OBAMA

In sincerity of heart, permit me to say that Africans should not expect anything from president Barrack Obama which is not in accordance with America's foreign policy. I have earlier stated that Obama is an American president, Africa should expect what they have expected from the previous American presidents. No doubt Mr. president has an African foundation, but that has not made him an African citizen. If Africans think that Barrack Obama would act beyond American constitution, such a person is one of the worst dreamers on earth. Everybody in this world migrated from a place, but the fact that the world is all about people's movement, such does not mean that an individual who has left his state of origin will still be carrying the passport, no! Life is not like that, president Obama is purely an American not an African president.

All Americans should throw their weight behind their president, because he will not fail, for he is aware of the expectations of the people of America. He is also very much aware that Americans are closely watching him to see if his policy on Africa will change from what Americans think of Africa.

Obama will not be the person that will change America's policy and politics to favour Africa, rather, what Americans will see is a close policy and politics of the former president Bill Clinton. All American presidents who were Israeli-Americans did not change the belief of America in the Middle East, all the Irish Americans did not change American policy and politics in Europe, therefore, Barrack Obama an African-American will not change the policy and politics of America in Africa. African leaders should go back to the drawing board, think and work, because Obama cannot leave his people to come down to Africa with American wealth to please them. Africa should not expect anything more from the president than they would from any American president. Becoming the first African-American president poses a stronger test on his loyalty and commitment to duty calls, extra effort must be put to work even more than past presidents to prove that African-Americans can be trusted. Being the first black president is enough responsibility for the president. All eyes all over the world are on him, not just Americans alone, both those who are for and against him, want to see his performance, and he will try his best to prove his critics wrong.

SPEEDY FIGHT AGAINST HUMAN RIGHTS ABUSES

Africans can only get things right if they can get up speedily and give a good fight against human right abuses. Nothing can work out politically when the level of human rights abuse is on the increase. On daily basis people of Africa are dying and humiliated by their fellow Africans who are fortunate to be in government. In Nigeria the level of human rights abuses is alarming.

Sometime in 2009, there was news of two men that were shot dead by the police, this was televised. The government only said they were going to investigate the incident even when they have all evidence on ground. In the same year, a young boy was killed by the police and the government did not do anything about it. There is what is called 'Apo six killing' in Nigeria. What is Apo six killing? Some few years ago six youths were massacred by the police in a village called Apo, an axis of Abuja, Nigeria's capital city. That matter is still in court to date. The reason is because the police are still investigating the incident, and also because the six victims were common Nigerians. The killing of journalists has become a tradition in our country, I cannot count the number of journalists that have been murdered by unknown gunmen, to date the police have not confirmed the arrest of any killer. The endless investigation is still going on. Political killings have scared many good people from joining politics in Africa. They do not want to lose their lives. The embarrassment and assault the Nigerian people are suffering in the hands of the police is no more a new thing to the people. In Nigeria anybody who calls the police for his foe is considered the worst enemy of such individual. A lot of people have died of police torture. Cases of torture have been reported times without number, still government is doing little or nothing to correct this evil on humanity. The police have killed thousands of innocent citizens in detention without trial to find them guilty by law court.

The judiciary is not helping matters. Armed robbers are now the real men on the Nigerian streets making life unbearable for citizens. The security system is inefficient. Unnecessary arrest of people without genuine reason is the order of the day, this is a serious and worrisome situation in Africa. Why are all these things happening? People get into government through the back door, undermining the fact that to be in government is a call to serve and protect the people, not for personal enrichment. It is dishearten to note that the seats of power are given to people who do not have vision for African countries. People with the highest level of greed, people with criminal intention, people who consider human blood as water. People who do not believe that tomorrow is very important to every one of us. People who see the seat of power as their private property, people who see the countries of Africa as their supermarkets. People who can deceive saints and make them murderers overnight. These leaders are the worst enemies of Africa. It is a pity that an African is not safe in African continent, what a story! African leaders will gather in a place to discuss peace for Africa, while lots of Africans who did not actually commit offence are suffering and dying in their custodies, some are being killed silently.

Ways to fight against human rights abuses include:

- Get good people with vision in government
- Put in place a formidable political structure
- Get better people involved in security.
- Equip the security sector properly and pay them well, mostly the police force.
- Let there be a law that government will sincerely monitor against human right abuses.
- Get people involved in the security of their lives
- Equip the judiciary properly
- Construct good prison yards and equip them well to avoid careless death in the cells
- Ensure that proper judgment is given based on fair hearing
- Make the police force attractive for intelligent people to enroll

MY VISION FOR AFRICA

The theme of this vision is 'Vision for all'. It is because the African child needs to be happy and have hope for a better tomorrow. Neglected African children need people who can help them give birth to their visions and ideas in life. African children do not want to be seen as baby soldiers anymore. The African child does not want to die of hunger anymore. African children need education like other children of the world. The African child does not want to die due to poor healthcare delivery. African children do not want to be separated from their parents anymore. The African child wants to be recognized by the government. The African child wants free movement in Africa. The African child does not want to die by stray bullets of the police anymore. The African child wants to go to bed and sleep to wake in peace without being harassed by gunmen. African child needs to be encouraged. I have a story for the African child:

I am a newly born chicken, I need my mother's wings to grow well. How important are my mother's wings to my growth? Very important! Without my mother's wings covering me my life will be exposed to danger, I will die young, I will be hungry and I will be tired of life. The earth knows that I am not strong, I am new to it, my legs are still very young, the earth knows that my mother's wings are the only protection I need, to have a future, to grow well, to eat well, to be strong enough to face the future, to think well, not to misbehave, not to fall sick, the earth knows all these, hence, I am pleading with you oh mother earth! Do not allow my mother to die. If she dies, oh mother earth! My vision will die with me as a chick, my future will die with me as a chick, my growth will suffer setbacks. If she dies, you too will not have me in the future. Hawks will carry me out of you, wolves will eat me up, my life will be in danger of wild animals. Please . . . please . . . oh mother earth! Do not allow my mother to die, for you need me as much as I need you oh mother earth!

The chick cries out in pains from the heart, for after the plea, mother earth still allowed its mother to die in torture. Oh! What a story of the young chick! Its future is shattered. Such is the story of the African child, mother Africa is crying in pains over the future of the African child. In politics everybody is supposed to be involved, because there is a saying that confirms every human as a political animal. Today, few people have seized the power of the people which is supposed to be by the people and for the people, thereby making nonsense of that wise saying. Everybody is not political animal anymore, rather, it is just a few people, while others are called political onlookers, and regrettably the African woman that is supposed to be honoured and respected is being abused and disgraced, making her cry daily without her husband and children.

Most African women are widows, because their husbands have been killed by politicians who wanted power at all cost. Most African women have lost their children who stood as their joy to endless wars and fierce politicking. A lot of women have been killed in the same intent, subjecting the hope of Africans to pains and torture. Women are the keepers of homes, therefore, African women should be welcomed to really participate in the building and development of Africa. Women should be allowed to play the role of mothers of Africa as it is. Women should be used to form a successful government. As a pastor of a small congregation, there were about 85% women in the church, and these women are the ones that support the ministry with inextinguishable love and without which the ministry will not survive. This underscores the importance of women. If I emerge the president of Nigeria today, I will form my government with women, because with the Nigerian women in my cabinet, we will erase Nigeria from the list of third-world countries. In a church where men are the first people to appear in a given service, except by divine favour, the church's growth will take a lot of time. Put women of vision in technical positions in your country and tell them what you want in a simple and no vague declaration, you will get quick result, because every mother has special feelings for her child. Women that are ready to work cannot take bribe for any reason, women that are ready to work cannot kill themselves for better result.

My vision for Africa is to strongly arouse leaders in the diversification of possible ways of generating revenue. Any government that has solely one channel of income is bound to fall. What happened to sector like agriculture? In the world's record, Africans are known for farm work, fishing, etc. What is wrong with the cocoa farm? Africa before the colonial days was the best producers of cocoa. What is wrong with rubber production? What is wrong with palm produce? In my village a lot of women used to make exorbitant sum from sales of palm oil. These are possible ways of lucrative earnings for the people and job creation. Banana plantation, is it an abomination? Government is very interested in quick wealth that does not improve the economy of the nation. Science and technology is dead, because the government has refused to bring better people on board to develop our technological sector. Africa, mostly Nigeria, has refused to industrialize, because there is oil in the Niger Delta region without which Nigeria cannot survive. The question is, can Africa ever develop without:

- Good roads
- Functioning energy sector
- Good water supply
- Housing for all, becoming a reality
- Agricultural reorientation programmes
- Industrialization
- Education
- Technological development
- Good political institutions and stable democratic structures
- Good transportation system (air, sea and land)
- Good trading relationship (local and international)
- Serious fight against human rights abuses?

These are my vision for Africa, and if all Africans will take these issues seriously, surely Africa must develop overnight.

How can all these be achieved?

Use the people to give them what they need and all of us will be very happy at the end. Government is a serious agent of motivation, when you get the people involved in the building and development of our future, allow the people to see the positive side of the government, make everybody part of it, only then will things begin to work well. When the people are involved and used to realize the vision one has for them as a leader, all these shall come into play:—

- Job creation
- Total eradication of poverty
- Development
- Free flow of government policies
- Sound health and sound living
- More hands will be needed for work
- Possible security/protection of lives and properties
- Reduction of crime
- Sufficient food
- Room for self employment
- Increased Tourism
- It will arouse patriotism among the people
- Democracy will truly be of the people, for the people and by the people.

MY MESSAGE TO AFRICAN FRIENDS

This is a very important message to all the friends of Africa, it is good to be called a friend, but more important is for such friend to tell himself a well deserved truth by asking and answering the following questions:—

- Am I a good friend to my friend?
- What kind of impact have I made in the life of my friend-positive or negative?
- Is my relationship with my friend based on dubious interest?
- Am I a friend that will tell his friend the truth that can move his life forward?
- Do I really love my friend?
- What do I really want to make out of this relationship, is it for my own personal interest or the benefit of both of us?
- Is this African friend of mine a dubious one who does not want the good of the people?
- What are my plans towards changing him if he is dubious?
- Will I be able to change this friend of mine?
- How can I be able to make him a giver instead of a receiver at all times?
- All the help rendered to this friend of mine, is he really using them well?

- What prospect do I have for my friend's house in the near future? (not clear)

These are the questions African friends should ask themselves and indeed provide candid answers to, because Africans are crying daily about the ills of corruption, and some foreign friends of Africa help them to cry over this faceless demon called corruption. As Africans and African friends are crying daily about corruption, we the people of Africa are realizing that most of these friends who cry against this unseen demon are the brain behind all these, they are the cause of this epidemic called corruption. Our oversea friends cannot tell us that my mother's shoes that were missing through my elder brother is found in his house, still he refuses to send them back because he feels his personal interest is making me and my family happy. Not at all, we believe that he is the one who is actually aiding my elder brother to steal from us every day.

How can African friends see that most of the things their friends do are based on criminality? African friends should know that whoever has the devil as his best friend is telling the world that indeed he shares something in common with the devil. I have heard of the money belonging to African governments that was illegally taken abroad, yet, these funds are still in oversea banks, and those countries where the money is deposited know that such illegality is going on in their countries, yet they sit on it in guise of investigating the source of such incomes. What a world! Deceit is the order of the day, people know what is right but they are not doing it.

African's oversea friends, how do you feel when the house of your friend is on fire and you allow him to relax in your house with troubles? We should rise and tell ourselves the bitter truth that can strengthen our relationship. Tell your friend who has come to hide in your house without putting out the fire in his house to go back home and take care of his burning home. This is appalling! You know that the president in power is a political criminal, yet, you did not tell him to leave the seat of power and put things right, rather, all you do is to form clique with such a person, you even visit him to discuss national issues. Is this not encouraging criminals in the government of Africa? Is this not killing African political structures?

It is welcoming what president Barrack Obama did when he visited Ghana and not Nigeria on his first visit to Africa as an American president. Ghana's political structure in Africa in recent times is the standard required of politics, and is of high class. The great man of America chose to visit Ghana, a country that is ready for change. But such action did not go down well with some Nigerians who are still very far from the truth, except a few who are ready to hear the truth no matter how bitter it is. Those few made it clear to people when some self deceiving ones asked, why the choice of Ghana instead of the giant of Africa? The reason is that the president of America cannot visit a country that is not ready for change. Weeks afterwards, the Madam Secretary Of State was sent to make Nigerians understand that there is what is called global change in politics, which means that Nigerians should take their destinies in their own hands. A lot of Nigerians asked questions that can never effect changes in the country. Questions that cannot change the criminality in the system, and the woman took her time to add that there is nothing anybody can do for Nigeria better than what Nigerians can do for themselves. This is a statement I consider a brilliant answer to the questions of the Nigerian people. Though some were good citizens, while some others were agents paid by the government to pretend like people that need help; actually they knew what they were doing.

Please Africa's oversea friends, look at the type of investments the people in power are putting up in your countries and tell yourselves if such persons have made such investment in their own countries before coming into power, investigate the investor, his past financial record then you will be able to see to it that Africans are suffering in the hands of Africans. What all the oversea friends of Africa should do for Africans is to forget all the evils of the past, help Africans fight against government financial corruption, and ensure that Africa becomes a true democratic region that can hold its own and manage her affairs without corruption, for then will Africans forgive and forget the ugly past.

Finally, all the countries that have at one time or the other played the role of colonialism in Africa should take a good look at the countries they colonized and see the level of corruption in those countries and try as much as they can to effect changes. If they refuse, let them place travel and investment embargo on those in government, both present and past. By so doing ordinary Africans will see that they are not supporting their unscrupulous deeds. What Africans need from their friends is to help us fight government financial corruption and help build a stable democracy as stated earlier, and ensure that corrupt people will no longer find their way to government house, this is the only way democracy can become truly government of the people, for the people and by the people.

CHAPTER FIVE

THE POWER BROKERS IN AFRICA

It is very important to note that Africa will forever remain Africa, it is even imperative to understand that the destiny of Africa is lying in the hands of Africans. It is very important for us to know that we cannot solve the problems of Africa without involving ourselves in the discussion that concerns us, we must involve ourselves in the school of discipline so as to ensure that correction is made. We must tell ourselves the truth about the past, because without us knowing much about our past in the areas we have erred and the areas we have done well, correction cannot be possible. The power brokers in Africa will have to accept the fact that they have failed the people and disappointed themselves. The power brokers in Africa must know that Africa is for Africans, not for them alone. They must know that we are special people that lack good governance, Africans are good people that lack good managers. Africans are good people blessed by God, and the power brokers subject them to suffering because of the interest of the few that surpasses that of majority Africans. The power brokers must know that for us to live for one another there must be changes in whatever we do. They must understand that there are global changes in governance meaning that fathers must allow their children to grow and take over leadership to bring about the realities of future hope. Any man who has children that cannot take over from him will suffer to his grave.

The power brokers in Africa are the problems of Africa, because they do not believe in global change, they do not believe in retirement, they do not believe that their time is over, that now they have to sit like fathers and see their children run around for them to make them happy. Africa power brokers don't believe that old age is a total blessing from God, they do not believe that the joy of a man is to see his children grow before him and start working to take good care of his old age, for that is my prayer as a father, I want to see my children grow and take over governance from me, to take good care of my old age, such will make me a fulfilled father. I want to see the Africans of tomorrow becoming good future leaders that will take over from us and continue from where we will stop. These power brokers lack what I call sustainable trust for themselves and for the youths of Africa, they do not trust themselves and will never trust the youths due to what I call 'ills of the past' that is reporting itself daily, making every one a suspect.

What are ills of the past?

In the days of colonialism, people were forced to believe in unrealistic unity, oneness and understanding. But all these were to favour the interest of the sacred cows in the merger. The colonial masters ruled Africans with suspicion thereby creating fear in the minds of Africans, the system was based on divide and rule.

What is divide and rule?

It is a situation where one Causes problems among people to get what he wants, thereby making the people to be in enmity with one another. The colonial days were the period wickedness was introduced to Africans, it was the time people from different backgrounds and cultures were brought together to live as one people caring less whether these people could afford to stay together or not, all that matter to the colonial masters was to satisfy themselves, and how Africans felt did not matter. As time went on, people started living in pretence trying to co-exist, suspecting one another, as such was part of colonization. We should consider it from three perspectives with examples of what has happened.

- Africans before colonialism
- Africans after colonialism
- What Africans need to move forward

AFRICANS BEFORE COLONIALISM

Africans before colonialism were hard working people who worked so hard to earn a living. Africans were known for their self reliance, they did not depend on anyone and they did not live without working. All the nations of Africa were known for one thing or the other which made them establish a lot of markets where they sold their goods and rendered services for humanity. These markets were only functioning in week days, for instance in my town, we had Afor market which comes up every four days, Nkwor, Eke and Orie respectively functioned alike. What the people produced those days were brought to be sold in these markets and it was paying them.

In Nigeria before colonialism, all the tribes were known for one thing or the other, the Igbo people were known for black smith, farming and palm oil production. The Yorubas were known for farming and cocoa production, while the Hausas were known for farming and cattle rearing. There were so many other nations like the Ijaw kingdom known for their fishing, Urhobo, Itsekiri, Benin kingdom, Tiv kingdom, Igala and so many other nations that make up Nigeria were known for farm and the production of mats, blacksmith, dry gin, caps, etc, and they were doing well taking good care of their people according to their cultures and traditions.

In ruling and governing people, each kingdom was operating monarchical system of government and there were no problems governing the people, because everybody was bonded {together} by laws according to traditions. There were no financial corruptions, because the kings who were the custodians of culture and traditions placed much value on them, for it was believed that whosoever that goes against the traditional values and laws would be killed by the gods of the land. It did not matter who such a person was, once the individual goes against the laws of the land such would die. The three arms of government were functional and effective, for nobody was ready to die in the hands of the gods.

The gods of Africa were serving as the legislature, the chief priests of the gods were the judicial officers in charge of interpreting the laws of the land to the people, while the executive arm of the government were made up of the kings and their palace chiefs. Whenever the kings erred the chief priests would react in accordance with the directives of the gods, and if it were ordinary citizens the priest would react as well.

Apart from the kings, there were village chiefs and elders. All the nations had different traditions and cultures, that is why what was allowed by the gods of these nations may not be allowed in other nations. In Ihiala kingdom, they had the king, the Ogbuefis (chiefs), the elders of the villages and clans called Okpara. There was the general god of Ihiala called Ulasi-miri alongside the chief priest and the king at the center, such was like the federal legislative arm of government. There were village gods and their priests as state legislators, the village chiefs were like governors, while elders were representatives and senators to the gods whose duties were to ensure that people placed value on the traditions and cultures. And there were seers who were like the prophets, they were members of the legislative arms of government, because they were working with the gods and the chief priests to see and speak for the gods. Africans had unwritten constitutions, still the laws of the land were highly respected, because people had great respect and fear for the gods.

DISPUTE SETTLEMENT

Before a case could be brought to the palace of a king, it had to be tried in other courts, because the palace of the kings and deities of the kingdom stand as the supreme court of justice, while the palace of the village chiefs serves as appeal court, and the palace of the eldest men stand as high court, while the clan chiefs were the low court. Any dispute that was not settled at the clan palace would be brought before the village head, if not resolved, might be forwarded to the palace of the king, but if it is a case that involves blood and law of the land the chief priest would be invited to the palace, because whatever decision taken at the palace would be taken to the deity where the chief priest would consult the gods over such matter. Whatever decision that will be taken on the matter stands as the last authority.

NATIONS AND THEIR IDENTITY BEFORE COLONIALISM

There are three major kingdoms in Nigeria and many minorities. I will only discuss the three major tribes, this is not to say that others do not have identities as in mode of dressing and title names.

THE IGBO NATION

The Igbo nation before colonialism was known for their belief which says 'Igbo enwe eze' meaning Igbo has no kings. This did not mean that the Igbo nation had no king. They did have kings, but they did not place premium on their kings like other nations. Every Igbo man believes in his ability to make wealth, because they are very enterprising. In Igbo land, everybody is empowered and this makes them independent, sometimes, making them to disrespect the rich, but that does not mean they do not believe in their traditions and cultures. He is well cultured. The Igboman is known for his strong belief in culture and traditions. He, like his counterparts from other kingdoms are well-cultured. However, as a result of his entrepreneurship he hardly respect the rich and it is this attitude that has led to the misconceptions and misinterpretation of these titles below

- Eze or Igwe—king
- Ogbuefi or Ichie—high chief

- Ezenwanyi—queen
- Lolo—wife of a chief
- Dara, Onowu, etc—low chief
- Okpara, Diokpa—eldest man
- Adah—first daughter
- Okeibiri—married woman
- Agadi nwanyi—old woman
- Agadi nwoke—old man

There is a way the Igbo nation is recognized and addressed, and there are other kingdoms in Igbo nation that have different ways of addressing the people.

Marital Rites in Igbo Land

When it comes to marriage in Igbo land it is a serious issue. Before colonialism much importance was attached to marriage, but it has diminished due to what they called civilization. Before now, the Igbos did not get into marriage through friendship. That was the reason why marriage and women were taken very seriously. Before colonial days, marriage in Igbo land did start from:

1. The family of a man who wants to get married would go to relations and friends to tell them that they are looking for a good lady from a good home for a wife for their son. The people informed would then start looking out for a lady from a good home as requested.

2. When a woman is eventually found the family of the man who wants to marry would be alerted.

3. The man would then visit the family to see the lady and her people. This kind of visit is usually referred to as let me see for myself or passer-by visit. It goes with a bottle of dry gin.

4. On arrival, the family of the lady must have been alerted by the middlemen that are bringing the visitors, so the family would present kola nuts and alligator pepper to the visitors, after which the visitors would present the dry gin to make their intention known.

5. The host would then call his daughter to come and pay homage to the visitors, this is after the mother must have told her the intentions of the visitors. For the lady to come out means she wants to see her proposed husband and for the man to also see his wife to be. The host would tell his visitors to go back home and repeat the visit later to afford them quality time to thoroughly ask their daughter questions concerning their visit. Agreement would be reached upon their return in two weeks time which is called 'Izunese'.

The visitors would repeat their visit on the agreed date to hear the result of their last visit and to know if the lady accepted them or not. The family would ask them to continue their visitation as they investigate the man who wants to marry their daughter to find out things like: what does he do for a living, the family background, etc. but in a situation whereby the man does not like the lady, they will not repeat the visit. Both families would engage in this investigation to find out the background of each other before the marriage would finally come up. If anything contrary to customs and traditions is discovered about any of the family at the time of inquiries, the relationship would be called off. But if otherwise, the prospective groom would come with two bottles of dry gin and a keg of palm wine to finalize the rites.

The final marriage rites in which the man would provide all required items demanded by the lady's family would include things like kola nuts, palm wine, alligator pepper, etc. Thereafter it will be made public. This is not a general law in Igbo land, because every kingdom in Igbo land has their laws on marriage, the giving of list differs from kingdom to another. The four days journey is for the bride to be able to know the bridegroom and his people, including the environment that would eventually become her home. During the four days journey the bride would be tested in many ways on all areas of life to know how ready she is for marriage. She would be tested to know:

- How hospitable she is
- How she can manage a home
- How she can keep environment clean
- How well she cooks
- If she has good manner of speech
- If she is a lustful person
- If she is quiet or radical

- If she does steal
- If she is a pretender
- If she is a troublesome woman
- If she is easily provoked.
- If she is hard working

These and other related characters are what the parents of the man would try to find out about the lady. As the prospective groom and his people are trying to know and perhaps understand the bride, her parents on the other hand would be doing a similar research about their likely son-in-law.

- If he is a jovial person
- If he is responsible
- If he is caring
- If he is capable of protecting their daughter
- If he is a complete man
- If he is industrious

These were some of the physical things the bride's parents would try to know about their would-be son in-law. They would make effort also to know the spiritual state of the man and his destiny, if at the end of this rigorous research they find him satisfactory, marriage proper would take place. This condition is not for all Igbos, because people live and behave in line with their customs and traditions, this is because Igbos and other nations in Nigeria worship diverse gods, that is why every of their social behaviour and cultures were as directed by their gods through the chief priest.

Concerning the lives of other nations in Africa, they live and behave in accordance with the culture and traditions of their land, both socially, morally and otherwise. There were different gods, traditions and cultures in Africa, hence, every ethnic group in Africa live and behave in line with their beliefs. The people of Nigeria is test case in this book because the characters of Africans before the arrival of the colonial masters are related to each other, though not exactly the same.

THE POLITICS AND LEADERSHIP IN AFRICA BEFORE THE VISITORS

Nigeria will stand as our view point to other African nations in this historical study to enable us get to the root of the whole matter. The reality of the Nigerian history has shown that there were well organized autonomous societies even before the advent of the European colonial power. Prominent among them were the Itsekiri, Benin and Oyo in the forest belt, the Igala, Jukun, Tiv and Nupe in the Niger Benue confluence regions, while the Hausa states and Borno are in the savannah region.

YORUBA KINGDOM

As long as history remains with man events will continue to unfold itself, because human race cannot live and succeed without historical memories. The Yoruba kingdom has been the dominant group on the west bank of the Niger. They are of mixed origin and were the product of assimilation of periodic waves of migrants who evolved a common language and culture which determines a complete and total nation on its own. The Yorubas were organized in perinea descent groups that occupied villages, communities and subsisted on agriculture, but from about eleventh AD, adjacent village compounds known as 'Ile' amalgamated into a number of territorial enclaves as loyalties to Ife clan became subordinate to allegiance to dynastic chieftain. This transition produced an urbanized political and social environment that was accompanied by a high level of artistic achievement, especially in terracotta and ivory sculpture and in sophisticated metal carving, produced at Ile-Ife. The brass and bronze used by Yoruba artisans were significant items of trade, made from copper, tin and zinc imported either from North Africa or mines in the Sahara and northern Nigeria.

The Yoruba placated a luxuriant pantheon headed by impersonal deity called Olorun and as well included lesser deities of which were once mortals who performed variety of cosmic and practical tasks. Oduduwa which was one of them was regarded as the creator of the earth and the ancestor of Yoruba kings. For every uniqueness put in play, a model is made by the effect it has on mankind. One of the creation myth hold it that Oduduwa was the founder of Ile-Ife and that he did not stop at that, but dispatched his sons to establish other cities where they eventually reigned as priest-kings and as well presided over cult rituals. Formal traditions of this type have been interpreted as poetic illustrations of historical process by which Ile-Ife ruling dynasty extended its authority over Yoruba land. These stories were attempts to legitimize the Yoruba monarchies after they had supplanted clan loyalties by claiming divine origin. More factual is the fact that Oduduwa initiated political centralization by supporting and preceding over aboriginal groups. His era experienced overwhelming political economical social and craftsmanship changes. The landmark achievement no doubts gave him strength and good face before the people who admired and adored his skillfulness at achieving his success. You'll agree with me that the hand of the allegiant bears rules, hence, they could not contain their love for him, they made a god of him.

Ife was the center of over 200 religious cults where traditions were manipulated for political advantage by the Ooni (king). Ife also lay at the centre of a trading network with the north. The Ooni supported his court with tolls levied on trade, tributes exacted from dependencies and tithes due to him a s a religious leader. Perhaps, the greatest legacy to modern Nigeria is in its artistic production of glass beads, terracotta figurious and political centralization and Ife science.

In matters relating to ascendancy, the Ooni was chosen on a rotation basis, especially from one of the several parts of the ruling Ife science dynasty, consisting of a clan of several thousand numbers. Immediately an Ooni is elected and crowned, he goes into seclusion in the palace compound and would not be seen again by the people except the need arises in an important occasion. In the state hierarchy after the Ooni, comes the palace officials, town chiefs and rulers of outlaying dependencies. The palace officials were the Ooni's spokes persons, they were elective and depended on the broad support of the community and admonition of the Ife oracle. Each official was chosen from the eligible clan members who had hereditary right to the office. Members of the royal dynasty were often assigned to govern dependencies while the sons of the palace officials assumed lesser roles as functionaries, bodyguards to the Ooni, and as judges.

During the fifteenth century Oyo and Benin surpassed Ife in political and economical powers, although, Ife preserved its status as a religious centre even after loosing power. Till date the Yorubas still have respect for Ooni priestly function and recognition of the common tradition of the Yoruba ethnicity is not wavering. The Ooni of Ife was recognized as the senior political official not only among the Yoruba, but also at Benin. He conferred Benin's rulers with the symbols of temporal power. The Ife mode of government was adopted at Oyo where a member of its ruling dynasty consolidated several smaller city states under his control. A council of state, the Oyo mesi eventually assumed responsibility of naming the Alaafin (king) from candidates proposed from the ruling dynasty and acted as a check on his authority. Oyo developed as a constitutional monarchy, but in actual sense, government was in the hands of Bashorun (prime minister) who presided over the Oyo mesi. The city was situated 170 kilometers north of Ife and about 100 kilometers north of present day Oyo. Unlike the forest bound Yoruba kingdoms Oyo was in the savannah and drew its military strength from its calvary forces which established hegemony over the adjacent Nupe and the Borgu kingdoms and thereby developed trade routes further the northern part.

In the first half of the nineteenth century the Oyo kingdom finally took a down trend and it crash landed. Oyo refugees established successor military states southward. The most popular of the states was Ibadan which eventually changed the ascendancy traditional values to throne, from royal connection to achievement in battles, a form of military autocracy.

The political organization of the Yoruba kingdom was developed in such a way that each had a descent-line which was in charge of his own quarter of the town. All the descent lines sent representatives to chiefs who owed their positions to their birth. These chiefs, usually known as the Iwerafa, had important political power of decision, but it was seldom the work of Iwerafa to take action on decisions. Political action as distinct from political decision, was the duty of the Oba and his administration. This formed another aspect of the Yoruba system. This consisted largely of the servants and messengers of the Oba. They took their orders only from the king. It could also consist of men who belong to one cult or the other. It would be the task of one or other age set to carry public works and perform services of value to the whole community. Inside the towns, it was the duty of the various heads of descent lines to look after purely local affairs.

In practice, the system was more complicated than any brief description could show, but the main point to grasp here is that the growth of power among the leading families greatly modified the segmentary pattern of local government. Though democratic in small matters, Yoruba government is different from Igbo government in being aristocratic, wherever important decision was concerned, power in big matters always rested in the hands of a minority of nobles. Government of kings and nobles makes it possible to unite the people of each main town firmly together, but impossible to unite the different towns. Each town's nobles tended to feel themselves in rivalry with those of neighbouring towns, even through the Ebi family system, as mentioned above, made all parts of the town the same big Yoruba family.

It should also be remembered that the Yoruba system, in this respect like other systems, rested not only on the political powers of appointed rulers among leading families, but also on their religious power. In the distant past, all the Yoruba states have great loyalty to the ancestors of Oduduwa and so to the

Ooni of Ife who was the senior living representative of those ancestors. But as civilization flowered and grew and the Yoruba population became more numerous, this common loyalty to Ife proved difficult to maintain. Each state tended to split its own loyalties, and to worship the spirits and gods in its own separate way. These are the reasons some of the leading Yoruba spirits and gods have taken different forms. In some places, for example, Oduduwa is more thought of as a man and in other places as a woman. Here, even more perhaps than elsewhere, religion and politics have always gone hand in hand.

BENIN KINGDOM

Broadly speaking, the term Benin has wide range of meanings. The term described the kingdom, the empire and the people situated in the forest belt in southern Nigeria, the ancient Benin kingdom posses conflicting traditional accounts of its origin, which was not asserted by the earliest version of the kingdom's origin. Recorded in 1823, it attributed the origin of Benin to a white man from the great waters who built the kingdom, if the account is anything to go by, it probably refers to early European visitors who came to Nigeria. From the creation myth, Benin had been where they were since inception. The myth holds that the youngest son Osamobua that came from heaven, taking with him a handful of sand and seal to work with and thus turned this water logged area into earth for his purpose. Some historians including Egharevba, the famous Benin historian, claim that Benins migrated from Egypt having stopped over for a brief time in Sudan. One other tradition linked them with Ile-Ife. The tradition posits that Onibini was one of the children of Oduduwa, this tradition is supported by yet another tradition that says Oranmiyan (Oranwanwe) in Benin tradition was a prince of Ife who reigned in Benin during the period of interregnum. Oranmiyan was said to have named Benin when he couldn't settle the dispute between the several lineages, hence, he refered to the place as Ile Ibinu-land of anger. This same tradition holds it that Ile Ibinu was relegated to Ibinu and Ibinu was corrupted to Benin (Bini)

The use of beads and other royal regalia as well as bronze work were introduced to Benin from Ile-Ife. It is not easy to say with precision the origin of the Benin people. What is certain is that the people of Benin and Yoruba have a lot in common. Inter marriage and cultural diffusion has further reinforced whatever the nature of any relationship.

The founders of the empire of Benin, like those of the Yoruba states, lie deep in the forgotten past. It seems that the first rulers of Benin, a trading settlement and afterwards a city of the Niger-Delta, acquired their powers soon after the forming of the first Yoruba states, or perhaps at about the same period. Tradition knows them as the Ogiso dynasty or line of kings. There is no doubt that the Edo people of Benin took some of the political ideas from their Yoruba neighbours. Traditions say that hundreds of years ago (probably about 400 AD) the Edo of

Benin became dissatisfied with their rulers. They accordingly sent to Ife and asked Oduduwa for one of his sons to rule over them. He sent them prince Oraniyan (or Orunyon), and Oraniyan started a new period in the political life of the Benin state. This does not mean, of course, that the Edos took over Yoruba ideas wholesale. Even if there was a close connection between the rulers of Benin and those of the Yoruba states, the Edos were very much a people with ideas of their own, we can see this in many ways. Their artistes, whether in Benin itself or any other Edo towns, were especially brilliant in their skill of working metal and evolved many styles of great distinction.

Written down not too long ago by chief Jacob Egbarevba, the royal traditions of Benin speak vividly of this period. One of the most famous Obas of this time of expansion was Ewuare, who came to the throne in about 1440, he was said to have traveled widely in Guinea and have visited the Congo. Ewuare was powerful, courageous and wise, the traditions say. He fought against and captured 201 towns and villages in Ekiti, Ikere, Kukurku, Eka and Ibo country. He took their rulers captive and he caused the people to pay tributes to him. He made good roads in Benin city, in fact, the town rose to importance and gained the status of a city during his reign. It was he who had the innermost and greatest of the walls and ditches made round the city, and he also made powerful charms and had them buried at each of the nine gateways of the city to act against evil charms which might be brought by people of other countries in order to injure his subjects.

It was under Ewuare too that the empire of Benin had its first sight of the Europeans, for in 1472 the Portuguese captain Ruy de Siqueira brought a sailing ship as far as the bright of Benin. However, Ewuare is remembered as an outstanding ruler not only for his conquests, but also for his contact with the wide world. He also presided over important political developments. It was under Ewuare according to tradition, that the state council of Benin was formed, together with other new political institutions, and it was from this time that the imperial system of Benin acquired not only a central government, but officials and developments and regular means of administering the empire.

Another ruler that came out of Benin kingdom was Oba Esigie. Changes were carried further under Esigie who came to power in about 1504 and added Idah, a state lying between Benin and Benue, to the empire. Esigie is especially remembered for having taken several important steps in transforming political power in Benin from the bases of ascription to that of achievement from men who wielded power, that is, simply because they were members of nobles families, to commoners who were appointed to positions of power by reason of their service to the king. Esigie is also remembered as the Oba who entered into good relations with Portuguese envoys who were arriving more frequently on his coast, missionaries also came from Portugal and were all well received. This Oba is remembered as a man of learning and having practiced astrology (Iwe-Uki), forerunner of the science of astronomy, the study of the stars.

He is said to have reigned for nearly half a century. Benin itself is now a city of great size, wealth and distinction.

Orhogbua followed Esegie in about 1550, Ehenbguda in about 1578 and Abuan in about 1606, all the three are praised in the royal traditions as sensible and forward looking rulers. The memory of Oba Ahuan being especially honoured as a herbalist and skillful maker of charms. In 1553, during Oba Orhogbua's reign a Portuguese who was with them wrote afterwards that the Oba (like Esigie before him) could speak, read and write Portuguese.

ITSEKIRI KINGDOM

The Itsekiri are coastal people who have settled around the creek for several centuries. To its west are the Yorubas in Ondo state, at the north was occupied by the Binis, to the east are the Urhobos, while to their south are the western Ijaws. Culturally, the Itsekiris who are said to be the founder of Warri in western Delta` have cordial relationship with the Edo of Benin and their Yoruba neighbours. The Itsekiris have diverse traditions of origin. Some trace their ancestry to Ode somewhere in Ijebu area, while some hold it to Benin origin, automatically this indicates that we have different layers of settlers. However, creation myth holds the root of the Itsekiris to be descendants of Umale, their deified and venerated ancestor. Despite the myth ofconflicting traditions of origin, the account of the ruling dynasty is factual.

Ginuwa, the founder of Itsekiri migrated from Benin with his entourage to Ode, which he however considered to be the capital of the new settlement. From this same settlement, Gbolokposo, Obrodo, Erere and Olume was founded by the princess of Warri having moved out of it. Historical records hold that the Itsekiris later migrated to the lower Benin river so as to benefit from the developing salt industry, moreso, to have contact with the Europeans who had moved to Benin for decades along the Benin river.

JUKUN KINGDOM

Like several kingdoms, the Jukun kingdom also has conflicting accounts ofits origin. One ofthe accounts says that they migrated from north-east to Nigeria along with the Borno people from Yemen and eventually went their different ways as a result of frequent rifts. Modern historians are of the opinion that they migrated from the Nile region, especially when consideration is given to the cultural and political affinities between the Jukun people and Egyptians. Jukun state of Kwararafa was traditionally one of the banza (impure) states in Hausa land. The kingdom was located in the Benue region, around Ibi, which thrived until the eighteenth century. However, between mid thirteenth and sixteenth centuries there was domination by the neighbouring Hausa states, hence, it paid tribute to Kano in the fourteenth century and to Zaria under the powerful queen Amina in eighteenth century. Jukun rose to the level of political eminence as a result of the twist and turn in the political fortune of Hausa land in the sixteenth and seventeenth century, for they constantly raided across Hausa land they subjugated the riverside later and ridiculed the power of Borno.

The rise of Jukun kingdom in the second half of the sixteenth century among other factors owed it to the death of queen Amina of Zaria, hence, creating leadership vacuum in Hausa land. Coupled with interval dissention within Hausa land leading to political division, thereby exposing the Hausa states to constant military exploits from Songhai to the west and Borno to the east, Jukun leaders capitalized on this loopholes to strengthen their empire. They evolve efficient and highly centralized political administration around this period. There was Aku, who yielded religion and political powers, his political authority was however limited. His councilors under the leadership of Abu who acted as a form of prime minister, exercised imminence check on the power of the Aku. Incidentally Jukun was not interested in building an empire, they raided their neighbours and allowed them to recuperate in a manner that has been described by local traditions that the 'Jukun only touch and go'. They did not establish hegemony over many of their richen part of the natural creation, yet, another tradition says that Nupe was an agglomeration of various groups that had migrated up stream from Idah with their leader Tsoede. The kuta say that they are immigrants from the north to the south and yet the Gbedji contend that they were originally Yorubas but elected to come under the rule of Tsoede, alias Edegi, the hero of Nupe people.

In order to understand the history of Nupe, it is necessary to undertake a biographical study of Tsoede, the pivot of Nupe history. He united Nupe people and won for them independence from Igala.

He was born in the middle of fifteenth century to an Igala prince and a daughter of chief Nku. Prior to his birth, his father was recalled to Igala to be a new king-Attah of Igala. Coincidentally, in the later years Tsoede was sent to Idah as a slave tribute of the royal house of Nku, but was recognized by his father as a result of the ring and charms which his wife gave to him as a present for the yet unborn Tsoede. Tsoede however became the favorite of his father, the Attah of Igala, moreso, being the only person that volunteered to climb a very tall palm tree to pluck the only fruit that could cure his father of a terrible sickness. The infinite love of his father for him attracted the displeasure of his half brothers who aimed at his life at all cost. Hence, the Attah advised him to flee to Nupe. From Idah, Tsoede Edegi fled to Nupeko and declared himself the ruler of the town with his twelve companions. Tsoede adopted a region political title called Etsu. He embarked on expansionist policy which was facilitated by considerable forces of the Calvary he had built. Tsoede was said to have brought the first sets of blacksmith, bronze casters and glass makers from Idah land and pioneered the technical expertise for canoe building, for war and trade. In the aspect of culture, he introduced bride price and the use of human sacrifice to the gods.

NORTHERN KINGDOM

Trade was the key to the emergence of organized communities in the Sahara region of Nigeria. Prehistorically inhabitants, adjusting to the encroaching desert were widely scattered by the third millennium B.C. when the desiration of the Sahara begun. Trans-Saharan routes linked the western Sudan with the Mediterranean from the time of cartage and with upper Nile from a much earlier date, also establishing an avenue for communication and cultural influence that remained open until the end of the nineteenth century. By this same routes, Islam made its way through south into west Africa after the ninth century A.D. by then a string of dynastic states stretched across the western and central Sudan. The most powerful of these states were Ghana, Gao and Kanem which were not located within the boundaries of the present day Nigeria, but which nonetheless, had an indirect influence on the history of the Nigerian Sahara. Ghana declined in the eleventh century but was succeeded by Mali, which consolidated much of the western Sudan under its imperial rule in the thirteenth century. Songhai emerged as an empire out of the small state of Gao in the fifteenth century. For a century, Songhai paid homage to Mali, but by the last decade of the same century it had its independent and brought much of the Malians domains under its imperial way. Although, these little empire had little political influence on the savannah state of Nigeria before 1500, they had a strange cultural and economic impact that became more pronounced in the sixteenth century especially because these states became associated with the spread of Islam and trade. In the sixteenth century moreover, much of northern Nigeria paid homage to Songhai in the west or to Borno, a rural empire in the east.

In Hausa land, the emergence of states appears to have been closely associated with the foundation of the great birane, as centers of political power and capital cities. The Bini of Hausa land which has a different political system from the Garri, has the seat of a new type of political powers. Of course, the Bini like the Garri had its own government necessitated by the organizational requirements of urban life. This government eventually became very complicated with power invested in a whole hierarchy of specialized officials, whose titles were still preserved in the local government terminology of Hausa land (e.g. Magajin geri, chief of the town, perhaps general administrator, Sarkin kasuwa, king of the market, sarkin rofa, gatekeeper, Mai-unguwa, ward head, president of immigrant communities such as sarkin turawa, chief of the Arab trading group in Kano, etc.) but over all was the authority of the sarki who also had his seat in the city. This sarki was not sarkin Bini but sarkin kasa, king of the country, which consists not of the Bini and its farm land but a large tract of surrounding territories containing many genuruwa and kauyukay all of which recognized the superior political power of the serki in the city. This was the form of political relations and structure in Hausa states.

The government of this type of state is central in the person of the serki and was essentially vested in a particular family, but it was not a simple hereditary autocracy. First, it was essentially feuded in nature, the power of the king depending on the degree to which he could command, this service of supporters of his authority. Also this degree in turn is dependent on the wealth of the sarki which could be used for rewarding his supporters, and on the needs of potential supporters which they might expect that the sarki could meet for them. Wealth lay in land, in its produce, and in its inhabitants.

To be successful, the sarki was required to surround himself with people serving him, (with military support and with assistance in the control of wealth-producing territories) in return for rewards (territory held as fiefs). This government therefore, was by a king and fiefs holding officials. The later might in some cases belong to royal lineage yan sarki, sons of the king, but generally they did not, their relationship with him being a feuded one, not one of kingship.

Far from being a hereditary autocracy, this type of government was the one where the power of the king rested on the maintanace of a delicate balance between the interest of the sarki on the one hand and the fief holding mesu sarauta on the other. Even the hereditary principle was qualified by the emergence of powerful officials as kingmakers. Observe that the royal lineages many collateral branches and choice of sarki's successor from among many claimants, reflected the balance of the limitations on the independent power of sarki as a distribution of fief holding officers, tended to become hereditary.

Finally, the establishment of this new form of government entailed a substantial recognition of society. New territorial groupings-the state emerged and in addition, new classes. In the old villages, permanent class distinction can hardly have a rising authority within the family group mainly being a matter of age. Now in the states, however they developed a sharp distinction between rulers and subjects, between mesu sarauta on the one hand, and talakawa (people holding no official position) on the other. The way in which the talakawa could enter the ruling class in view of development of fief holding lineages were very few. There is an indication that this was sometimes achieved as a reward for outstanding military service. With the development of the sarki, there grew up a class of palace official fadawa who could be of ba-talake origin. Again, there is evidence of eventual emergence of class of slave officials obviously recruited from the talakawa. But generally, the society of the states appears to have lacked mobility between political classes.

The political changes associated with the emergence of Islam as a political force in Hausa land led to many changes in government in the great Hausa states. In Katsina, this association is clear and simple, besides being the first muslim sarki, Mohamad Korau was a founder of a new dynasty of Katsina-Laka origin which replaced the kings of the Durbawa whose descendants holding the office of Durbi eventually sank to the level of subordinate-mesu saraute. The new rulers, the Wangarawa founded Birmin-Katsina whose walls are said to have been built by Ali Murabus.

In Zazzaus (Zaria) the praise significance of the reign of Mohamed Rabbo is not clear, but here also, within a decade of his death, dynastic changes appeared to have taken place. The twenty second sarki was Bakwa Turunku (reigning at the end of the fifteenth century). This name is usually believed to mean the stranger from Turunku, and if this is correct it may indicate that the main political power in Zazzau passed at this time from the ancient line to the descendants of dynasty of Turunku. This reign is traditionally regarded as opening a new era of political development in this state. The political changes was said to have important repercussions in the rest of Hausa land.

MY POSITION ABOUT THE STATELESS STATE OF IGBO NATION

Many historians have one thing or the other to say about the Igbo governance and all they are saying is anchored on the belief that, Igbos are stateless nation due to the fact that Igbo governance starts from their families, lineages and clans. Every nation in Africa believes in extended family ideology which made it possible for them to be able to implement the laws of the gods in the ancient days. Tracing the migration of the Igbo nation, it has provoked a lot of views among the people, they have come to terms with the fact that Igbos migrated from Israel. Igbos are the Jews that left the land of Israel when God scattered the Jews abroad and they left but stopped over at Ethiopia. Eri who was also known as Njimofor and some others left Ethiopia and continued their journey stopping over at many nations, due to their believe that they are the only children of God, they were unable to settle down anywhere. When they came down to western African sub-region some stopped over at Benin while some continued and those that stopped at Benin couldn't cope with the Binis, so they moved to join their brethren who had already settled down across the Niger, which later became eastern Nigeria. Before their arrival, the early settlers Eri (Nri Njimofor) had occupied the Anambra area while other warriors settled at Isiala Ngwa (present day Abia state). Till date Isiala Ngwa that claims to be the senior, Eri is also claming to be the senior, but the fact remains that before the arrival of the Jews it was Ngwa who claims to be the first to have settled on the land, while Eri is claiming to be the eldest. This argument is not factual, because it has no historical evidence. In the couises of study of the migration of the Igbos one realizes that Igbos are Nazaretans that scattered alongside their brethren when there was trouble in the land of Canaan. Until date, no exact date was given concerning the migration of Israel, this is why other kingdoms are finding it difficult to believe that Igbos are the Jews. However, there are some spiritual and physical link with the Igbo:

- Jews are very enterprising
- Jews are culturally and traditionally disciplined
- Jews are religiously inclined
- Jews are not on the peace making side when it comes to protecting their rights
- Jews are very stubborn and are ready to die protecting their interest
- Jews are not loved by their neighbours
- Jews are technologically inclined
- Jews are proud people and boldly confront challenges with their heads held high

These are the characters of the Igbos which made people feel Igbo do not show respect, neither do they believe in the leadership of anybody, for as a matter of fact every average Jew strive with everything in him to be self reliant, but that does not mean they rarely believe in leadership and good governance.

Tracing the leadership of the Igbo from the beginning and that of biblical Israel, you will discover that it is God that chose leaders for Israel from their families and decentralize leadership among them. For instance, David from the tribe of Judah was the king of Israel and God pronounced the tribe of Judah the king of Israel, while the tribe of Levi are chief priests that offer sacrifice to God, this is how it had been from onset. When the grandson of David (Rehoboam) disagreed with the people of Israel over taxation and other issues which caused division among Israelites leading to their parting ways, Jeroboam leaving with ten tribes of Israel and only two for Rehoboam, even with this account, this did not mean Israel is stateless, every family in Israel were well represented in the palace, because the head of every family stands as a leader in that family. The Nigerian Jews cannot be exceptional, if this claim is to be properly researched and original account is given to help trace the original history of ancient day Israel to investigate the traditions and cultures of the Igbos, then people will understand that Igbos are not stateless.

The Igbos, though divided into several cultural groups, were united in more fundamental ways. Like many other people in Guinea and elsewhere, they ran their affairs on what is called segmentary pattern. It will be useful to discuss, at least the principal ways in which segmentary systems worked, because they composed a significant aspect of historical politics in West Africa and other parts of Africa as well.

The best way to understand a segmentary government is to have a mental picture of one big family, from grandparents to grandchildren, who form a village and farm the land neareby. As time goes by, this family grows bigger, sons became fathers and grand children became grandparents. As this happens, the original family unit break up into a number of self-governing parts or segments, led by heads of new families within the groups. Nevertheless, all the families stay held together in common loyalty to their founding ancestors. This loyalty is maintained by the group's religious belief, by the shrines of their ancestors and by their understanding of how their ancestors wished them to behave. This belief gave force to laws of the village. Village government is held together by ties of kinship and religion.

Village government of this type had two main problems in their political life, the first was to know how to recognize their rulers from time to time, so as to take account of the rise of families as the population grew bigger, the second problem was to make sure that separate loyalties to different descent-lines were balanced by a common loyalty to the groups as a whole. These two problems are solved in segmentary system in which way differs much in detail but the same.

The solution to the first problem was to enable junior branches of a family to split away peacefully from the senior branches, acquire their own land, find a place of honour for their own (but now separate) line of ancestors, and generally fit quietly into the life of the neighborhood. This was done essentially, by ceremonies which transferred authority from the head of senior branches to the heads of junior branches who wanted to start a new and semi-independent life of their own. Other ceremonies allowed for splitting away or fission.

The main solution to the second problem or making sure that separate family royalties were balanced by common loyalty was found, as noted above in religious ties which joined these two families in respect for their common ancestors. But these ties could be reinforced in various ways, they might be reinforced through the formation of age set to which all the men and women belonged, or by special political associations whose leaders had power throughout the area of the government in question. Many village governments might also be joined together through religious ties and ceremonies, in respect of ancestors of still bigger units, usually called clans, Igbo land had many hundreds of clans products of a few village governments which had grown in sizes and split-up during the distant past, into many governments. This could be a disadvantage to them in time of danger from invaders, unlike people organized in big units under kings, they could not rely on big armies, but it also had an important advantage. It was extremely democratic. The segmentary system in Igbo and others like them were nothing if not popular government, every grown-up man could, and did have his say at village assemblies where matters of common interest were deliberated. Systems like these were good for individual development, people accustomed to a great deal of everyday democracy are people with great deal of individual self confidence.

Of course, the amount of democracy varied, some of the Igbo, like the Tiv, Konkonba, Tallensi and other people with village governments had much democracy. This was less among the Igbo who develop title societies such as those of Ama at Nsukka and Ozo at Awka. These were run by a minority of men who were rich enough to pay high fees for the privilege. The same was true among the Cross River Igbo whose Ekpe association functioned on the same principle. Yet, here again, the premium was put on individual ambition and enterprise. A system with political associations might be dominated by a handful of rich men, but it is always possible in the Igbo ruling system for other men to enter the group by hard work, and not, as in most systems ruled by kings, simply because they had been born into a ruling family. Promotion in other words was by achievement and not by ascription, in this way if not others, village governments of this type were much in line with the democratic habits of the modern world. All these help to explain why the people of the Igbo country, most of whom had segmentary governments of one kind or another, acquired a well founded reputation for enterprise in trade.

AFRICANS AFTER COLONIALISM

The empirical views above illustrated what Africans gained and lost to colonialism. It is in view of today's Africans that much would have been achieved through colonialism than what they have gotten. Looking around to see that the benefit of colonialism is much more visible as much as what Africans lost, for example, education is the key to civilization without which civilization is not in view and developmental process of life will never be in sight. Therefore credit is given to colonial masters on education. With education things like these have been achieved by Africans:

- Human development
- Socialism
- Empowerment
- Reasoning and thinking in the right direction
- Sidelining fetish system of living
- The end of ritual killings
- Introduction of technological means of transportation e.g. bicycle, car, train, etc.
- Modern system of governance (democracy)

These are benefits of colony masterminded by education which was a product of colonial masters. Africans also gained some modern leadership experiences, sidelining the monarchical system of governance. Africans will not forget in a hurry that without colony, academic strength would have been an oversight. Infrastructural development would not have been in place.

Nevertheless, Africans lost a lot, hence the adage: "If you do not loose, you cannot gain." It is in the lossing a lot that brought the ideas of gaining a lot, that is why when Africans cry over slave trade, I am of different view in this matter, for slave trade worked in two ways. It helped Africans to civilize, for most of whom were taken into slavery would have been rendered useless if they had been in Africa. Despite this fact, some would have been better off in Africa than what they are today, therefore, when one cries over what he has lost, let him look within to see if there are little gain out of the lost and console himself with it. Today, we have black people all over the world, such is the dividend of slave trade, because if most of them were born in Africa they would have probably been corrupt more than those we see today. But due to their relocation, though through forceful means which is crime against humanity, they received another orientation about what life is really all about, that is why they can now think and talk about corruption and kick against it without fear or favour of anyone. The issue of slave trade should be handled with every sense of humour and carefulness.

Now talking of the destruction of African cultural values and what Africans gained from foreign culture, it could be seen that Africans are doing what they want to do and therefore nobody should be blamed for it. Every country in this world fights to protect their cultural values except Africa. Africans are living on imitation, they cannot improve on what they have learned, instead they continue to copy. African cultural values have been buried in the grave with the ancestors, that is why a pretty African woman can walk in the street naked and call it civilization. African woman before colony has what is called self-respect, it is very difficult for one to see the nudity of an African woman. Marriage before colony is a thing of honour and admiration, it put bachelors and spinsters off balance, they all want to have experience. But today, African woman has lost her values and has become the cheapest commodity in the street because we have opted to replace our cultures with that of the foreign. To ponder on the days of our ancestors, one would cry over and over again for Africa. Men put their wives away at will, this is Un-African Indeed, this is not the culture of the Blackman.

Our local languages have been relegated to the background, if not completely done away with, because everybody wants to speak the tongue of another man's language. Due to negligence of our cultural values and practically adopted another's we have lost:

- Cultural food, which is herbs, vegetables and fruits
- Cultural dressing
- Moral behaviour
- Cultural dance steps
- Communication system

- Cultural games
- Platonic relationships that exist between opposite sex
- African feelings and concern for one another
- Sincerity to one another
- Cultural means of dispute settling among brethren
- Native language
- Cultural ways of marriage, etc.

Africans have killed and buried the aforementioned cultural values due to open arms we have shown to foreign lifestyle, which is considered foreign cultures. No colonial master would desire to live like Africans, rather, they will desire to inculcate in Africans their culture. Africans are to be blamed for the evil done to themselves. When we finished with the colonial masters, we expected that Africans would go home and develop what they learnt from colonialism, rather, they continued to live and improve on foreign cultures without considering the African environment and upbringing right from the ancestors to the present. Africans will continue to get things wrong, because they have allowed the seed of corruption to develop in them without having understanding of what they are doing to their future. Today, an African is considered the most notorious criminal in the world. Our ancestors were not criminals, rather they were robbed ignorantly, mother Africa is not happy seeing what is happening to this generation:

- Abuse of our children as child soldier
- Abuse of our women as harlots that sleep with animals

- The crimination of African man abroad
- African men dressing like women and women vise versa
- The tradition and culture of Africa was sold ignorantly
- Modern slavery
- Customary courts where women are harassed and molested in line with their male counterpart

Mother Africa is crying, her abode cannot contain her anymore, her children have messed up the culture and tradition of Africa she bought with her life and retained. Mother Africa is not happy.

ADVICE TO AFRICA

Let us make the sacrifice of declaring emergency on resettlement on African tradition and cultural values so that we could maintain a stand, locally and internationally. Let us take the advice of mother Africa which says Africans must behave like Africa. A Blackman must admire and cherish his complexion. African man must be proud of Africa. Think Africa, reason Africa, speak Africa, dream Africa and project Africa.

Let African friends who have interest of Africa at heart come together and help Africa to democratize and have good leadership, and make Africans understand the need of traditional and cultural values. Long live Africa and long live the colonial masters!

WAY OUT

I am of the opinion that all the countries that colonized Africa should go back and tell themselves the truth about what they know about Africa before the colonialism. They should come down to Africa and put up programmes that would make Africans come up like them politically, socially and otherwise. Stop supporting corrupt leadership in Africa by sanctioning dubious governments, lift visa bound on the people of Africa. Africans must be given sense of belonging if the world is truly a global village. Racism must be treated with every sense of urgency. These and a host of others should be done if the world wants Africans to forget the ugly past, because the past is a very bad story that should not be told in the future.

WHAT AFRICANS NEED TO MOVE FORWARD

The people of Africa need to accept their fate in every area of life so as to recall their traditional and cultural values that have been destroyed. Unless Africans realize that there is need to think, dream and visionalize Africans before colony, how our fathers failed, the areas they made progress and the areas they failed, proper corrections will not be possible. Africans need to forgive one another and totally do away with foreign cultures that have deceived them, otherwise, total independence of Africa will not be in view. Today, in the world of the black nations, people want to run away from their fathers' land, because it is not modernized, and migrate to another man's land that is well built forgetting that whoever that fails to put his house in order will never have a positive future. Today, it is difficult for an African child to speak the language of his father, because someone somewhere has succeeded in making him see his father as a foolish man.

Do Africans really want to stop begging? Do Africans really want to know what it means to develop? Then, what is the home oriented programmes which speak Africa for Africans? Africa lost it all when she was defeated long ago to take away the values of the black man, and after the exit of the colonial masters, they refused to go back to history, instead, Africans tell history as stories, but have study in schools to acquire certificates that are useless outside the classroom. Does a Chinese speak another man's language? Does a Japanese speak another man's language? Does an Arabian speak another man's language? Do Indians, French, Germans, Briton, and even the Scandinavians speak another man's language? None of these countries aforementioned use another man's language as their national language that is why they are developed and still developing. Chinese people speak to themselves, think and reason together to improve their standard of living. Indians speak and hear themselves that is why they reason together to solve their problems. Arabians speak to themselves because they understand themselves, hence it is practically impossible for any opposition to break the Arab world.

The world of Africa after colony is the world of begging, they borrow the language they speak, because no African country uses their indigenous language as their national language, except a few Arab-African countries in the northern Africa who have refused to let their cultural and traditional values be taken away from them. Africans borrow drugs, because the people of Africa have allowed someone somewhere to tell them that the herbs which God said we should use for healing is now poisonous, forgetting that our ancestors whom some of them lived up to 200 years and above lived their lives thanks to herbal benefits. Africans borrow clothes leaving the original African attire. People die at the expense of deceitful civilization. There is nothing African people can boast of, apart from the mineral resources that God deposited in their land. Africa is blessed with fertile land, which means Africa is supposed to export food, but otherwise is the case, because agriculture is totally neglected. The reason is that God had deposited a lot of this minerals in the land of Africa, as such, the leaders are not thinking and reasoning in the right direction, because they lack vision for the people. Whoever that is going into power is not going there, because he wants to develop the country, rather, he is going in with one popular vision; to kill, to steal and to destroy the people, their tradition and cultural values. For a leader to steal, election will be rigged, because treasury must be looted and taken to unknown banks. To kill; the people who may want to oppose such move must be assassinated. To destroy; the strength of the Blackman must be weakened in order to subject him to the system of begging from year to year. These are the vision almost every African leader, both past or present have for Africans, except a few in the past like Nelson Mandela whom I see as the only African man, born by an African to live and die for the people he loves so much. Another, person is the ex-president of South Africa, Thabo Mbeki who decided to call it quit when he discovered that the people are not buying his ideas, he's a true African who was man enough to take decision like our ancestors. He was not politically corrupt, therefore, he had no time to shop for replacement, he had nothing to loose and he had nothing to gain instead when he discovered that people were not dancing to his kind of music anymore. Africans of old take good decision at the right time that was why most of our ancestors who rejected the colonial masters chose to die than see them destroy their tradition and cultural values which they inherited from their fathers. Today, no African leader is ready to resign from office because his ideas are not welcomed by his people. No African leader is ready to stand for a change, because he wants to remain a godfather, even when he is no more in power. If Nelson Mandela were a Nigerian, he would have ruled South Africa for life, perhaps, he would step down after two terms in office to continue as an unseen president from his home. He will still be the person to decide who rules South Africa and who won't, because he would want the people to see him as the most powerful man in South Africa. Nelson Mandela, Thabo Mbeki, John Kufur and Jerry Rawlins are political examples in Africa.

In conclusion, if Africa wants to move forward in all spheres of life, we must stop borrowing ideas that are not Africa-oriented. We must allow the ideas of the colonial masters that did not promote African heritage to die with their exit. We must come home to develop our mother language and use them in all African countries' as our national language. We must sit to talk to ourselves like Africans as we look at ourselves directly in the eyes like our ancestors did, and agree to be Africa, live in Africa and revive our cultural heritage which is not against the laws of God almighty. Long live Africa!

ABOUT THE BOOK

WHAT AFRICAN NEEDS: A book of indictment, correction and expository of politics and what true democracy is all about, it exposes African manner of leadership in copying other established countries of the world, privatizing democracy and seat of power, making good governance an illusion to African. What Africans need is equity and justice, fair play, understanding of who an African is and what African can do for Africans, making our foreign friends to realize that Africans are not fools, Africa before colony is far better than Africa after colony what we see today as benefit of colony is outright corruption and sit tight government which never wants a change.

Plundering African treasury, destroying the cultural values of Africa, making Africans to suffer and become slaves in their own father's land. what Africans need is a change of mentality, ideas, thinking , reasoning and understanding mind to allow better leaders to emerge and take Africans to their promise land.

That is what Africans need.